# ENTERTAINMENT INDUSTRY
## *The Business of Music, Books, Movies, TV, Radio, Internet, Video Games, Theater, Fashion, Sports, Art, Merchandising, Copyright, Trademarks & Contracts*

## MARK VINET

## WADEM PUBLISHING
### Entertainment Industry Association

## www.markvinet.com

Library and Archives Canada Cataloguing in Publication

Vinet, Mark, 1964-
    Entertainment Industry: The Business of Music, Books, Movies, TV, Radio, Internet, Video Games, Theater, Fashion, Sports, Art, Merchandising, Copyright, Trademarks & Contracts / Mark Vinet.

Includes bibliographical references and index.

10-digit ISBN 0-9688320-3-2
13-digit ISBN 978-0-9688320-3-5

1. Mass media-United States.  2. Mass media-Canada.
3. Arts-United States.  4. Arts-Canada.  5. Publishers and publishing-United States.  6. Publishers and publishing-Canada.  7. Intellectual property-United States.  8. Intellectual property-Canada.  I. Title.

PN1584.V46 2005          700'.973          C2005-904921-9

Artwork: www.proudproductions.com

For any additional information contact:

Mark Vinet
WADEM PUBLISHING
Entertainment Industry Association
117 Bellevue Street
Vaudreuil-sur-le-Lac, Quebec, Canada, J7V-8P3
Telephone: 450-510-1102 / 450-371-1803
Fax: 450-510-1095
E-mail:   mark@markvinet.com
Website:  **www.markvinet.com**

# AUTHOR

Historian and author Mark Vinet was born in 1964 in Sorel, Quebec, Canada. He is a fluently bilingual (English-French) entertainment and copyright lawyer, and, co-founder and former Executive Vice-President of MPV Entertainment (Kafka Records, Polliwog Festival, artist management, music/book publishing, entertainment e-commerce, recipient of several gold and multi-platinum records, ADISQ Félix awards, MIMI awards and JUNO nominations). Recipient of the "James McGill University Entrance Award" he obtained his law degree at McGill, was admitted to the Quebec Bar, and did post-graduate research work in the United States and Europe. Over the past 30 years, Mark has been involved in most aspects of the entertainment business in Canada, USA, and Europe. He began his career in music as a recording artist with Capitol/EMI and then switched to the business side of the entertainment industry while living in Los Angeles. He presently teaches college level courses in entertainment business, music history, contracts and copyright law. He currently is the host of an FM talk-radio program and practices entertainment law in Montreal.

Mark Vinet is founder of the Music History Association and the North American Historical Institute, which presents a series of his entertainment and history lectures. He is author of the books entitled *EVOLUTION OF MODERN POPULAR MUSIC: A History of Blues, Jazz, Country, R&B, Rock and Rap*; *CANADA AND THE AMERICAN CIVIL WAR: Prelude To War*; and the French language Civil War book entitled *LE QUÉBEC/CANADA ET LA GUERRE DE SÉCESSION AMÉRICAINE: 1861-1865*.


# DEDICATION

This book is dedicated to my parents – Judith Wade & Claude Vinet; my godparents – Lucie Vinet & Fernand Boutin; my maternal grandparents – Ellen Hewitt & Robert Wade; and my paternal grandparents – Blanche Poirier & Aldéric Vinet.


# ACKNOWLEDGMENTS

I wish to thank the many entertainers, entrepreneurs, authors, scholars, curators, and friends who helped me with my research for this book. My gratitude is extended to all those who warmly greeted and assisted me on my numerous field and research trips throughout North America and Europe.

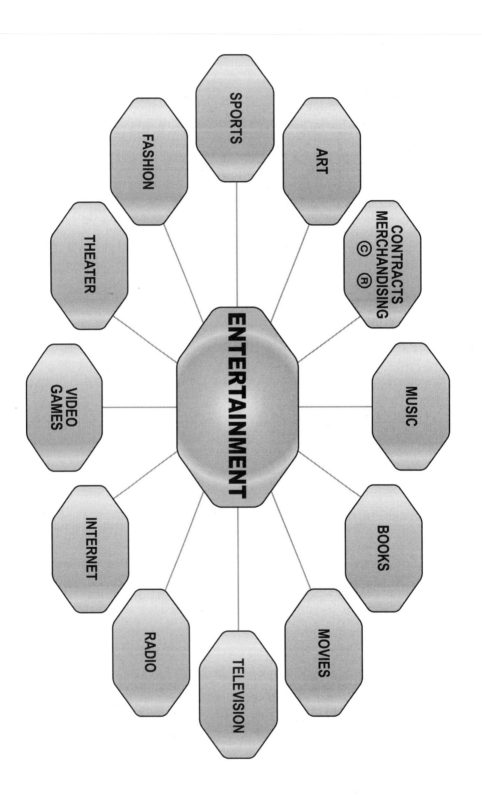

ENTERTAINMENT

- SPORTS
- FASHION
- THEATER
- VIDEO GAMES
- INTERNET
- RADIO
- TELEVISION
- MOVIES
- BOOKS
- MUSIC
- CONTRACTS MERCHANDISING ©  ®
- ART

# TABLE OF CONTENTS

LIST OF CHARTS ......................................... 6

INTRODUCTION .......................................... 8

PROLOGUE ................................................ 12

1.  COPYRIGHT .......................................... 15

2.  TRADEMARKS ........................................ 44

3.  ENTERTAINMENT DEALS & CONTRACTS ..... 56

4.  MUSIC ................................................ 64

5.  BOOKS ................................................ 77

6.  MOVIES .............................................. 86

7.  TELEVISION ........................................ 101

8.  RADIO ................................................ 109

9.  INTERNET ........................................... 114

10. VIDEO GAMES ..................................... 119

11. THEATER ............................................ 123

12. FASHION ............................................ 129

13. SPORTS .............................................. 132

14. ART ................................................... 135

15. MERCHANDISING ................................. 138

16. JOBS & CAREERS .................................. 140

EPILOGUE ................................................ 143

BIBLIOGRAPHY, NOTES & SOURCES .............. 144

INDEX ..................................................... 151

# LIST OF CHARTS

Entertainment Industry / 4
Entertainment Industry Tenets / 7
Intellectual Property / 14
Copyright Truths / 43
Trademark Ownership Symbols / 54
Entertainment Industry Truths / 55
Essentials of Entertainment Contracts / 61
Entertainment Contract Clauses & Provisions / 62
Music Industry / 63
Singer Musician / 67
Music Production / 68
Record Label / 69
Music Composer / 71
Music Publishing / 72
Key Music Industry Contracts / 73
Book Industry / 74
Book Writer / 75
Book Production / 76
Movie Industry / 85
Film Personnel / 97
Film Production / 98
Film Production "Behind The Scenes" Personnel / 99
TV Industry / 100
Television Production Personnel / 106
Television Programming / 107
Radio Industry / 108
Radio Formats / 112
Internet Industry / 113
Internet Infrastructure / 117
Video Games Industry / 118
Theater Industry / 122
Fashion Industry / 128
Sports Industry / 131
Art Industry / 134
Merchandising Industry / 137

# _ENTERTAINMENT INDUSTRY TENETS_

## UNDERSTANDING CONVERGENCE IS THE KEY TO SUCCESS IN THE ENTERTAINMENT INDUSTRY

———————

## TALENT EVENTUALLY REQUIRES THE INVESTMENT OF TIME, EFFORT, AND MONEY FROM STRANGERS

———————

## EVERY STEP IN THE ENTERTAINMENT INDUSTRY INVOLVES CONTRACTS,

## EVERY MOVE IMPLICATES COPYRIGHT

———————

## COPYRIGHT IS THE PRINCIPLE SOURCE OF POWER, CONTROL, AND MONEY IN THE ENTERTAINMENT INDUSTRY

———————

## IN ORDER TO GUARANTEE PAYMENT, ALWAYS POSITION YOURSELF SECURELY IN THE REVENUE FOOD CHAIN

### REVENUE FOOD CHAIN

CONSUMER
RETAILER
WHOLESALER
DISTRIBUTOR
PRODUCTION COMPANY
MANUFACTURER
ARTIST

# INTRODUCTION

The entertainment industry is a multi-billion dollar business that showcases the work, services, talent, and creativity of a cross-section of the international workforce. The modern entertainment industry is the convergence of the business of music, books, movies, television, radio, Internet, video games, theater, fashion, sports, art, merchandising, copyright, trademarks, and contracts. Opportunities, jobs & careers abound in this vibrant, eclectic, and exciting universe – open to anyone willing to learn and work diligently with creative enthusiasm.

To be on the cutting edge of this ever-changing industry, one must possess an in-depth knowledge of the many areas that converge to form modern show business. Entertainment lovers of all ages will enjoy this engaging overview of an evolving industry; from its basic and traditional roots to today's exciting technological innovations that rapidly and constantly influence the entertainment we enjoy. Experience a fascinating and enthralling odyssey while exploring dozens of artistic disciplines that can lead to success in the international entertainment field. A spotlight shines on specific business opportunities, crucial information, general knowledge, specific advice, and the art of negotiating entertainment deals and contracts. Discover the different types of jobs and careers available in the entertainment industry and the effective tools used to produce & market products. Discover the fundamental & essential provisions of publishing, copyright & trademarks, including deal-making and standard contracts used by professionals in the entertainment industry.

*ENTERTAINMENT INDUSTRY* is the second in a series of books dealing with the entertainment business by author, musician, radio host, entertainment lawyer, and historian Mark Vinet. It offers an in-depth study and detailed analysis of the eclectic, vibrant, colorful, and creative art forms that fill the leisure and recreational time of North Americans.

This book contains the author's personal entertainment industry rules, tenets, advice, principles, opinions, philosophies, and concepts developed over a thirty-year career in show business as an artist, musician, writer, performer, businessman, manager, and entertainment/copyright lawyer. For every rule or principle, however, there are numerous exceptions. Also, the charts presented throughout this work are generally complete but inherently subjective; objective additions, subtractions, and omissions to the structure of these charts should thus be considered and taken into account. No chart, however detailed, is perfect or fully complete. Each category included in the charts was judged to merit mention and attention. Most charts provide for one central topic and twelve components or categories in clock-like formation (wheel-like diagram/structure/design) randomly placed in no set order of importance or preference. The charts, by their very nature, flow inward and outward, automatically connecting all components. They are all intertwined, interconnected, and interrelated. The charts are thus a reflection of the true converging nature of the entertainment industry. Also, each component is potentially a world onto itself with its own sub-components or satellites. In other words, each business universe has many other universes within.

To better appreciate the contents of this book, certain specific terminology and abbreviations should be noted. For example, the term "North America" refers principally to the countries of Canada and the United States. Although some terminology and abbreviations are standard, others are custom-made and delivered by the author. The author believes that voluntary and conscious unorthodox use of the written language for the purpose of effect or emphasis is refreshing and stimulating.

The author has conscientiously chosen to employ capital letters, Italics, and punctuation marks to better present, organize, or emphasize certain passages of this book. Although the standard rules of spelling and grammar are not always voluntarily followed, one hopes this good faith explanation will merit a benevolent acceptance and appreciation from you the reader.

The author's goal was to make this book enjoyable to write and read, or in other words – a book written to be read. To this end, the author elected to write a book he himself would take pleasure in reading. He strongly believes that books should be savored and enjoyed by all, not only academics, scholars, and professionals. Small print and distracting footnotes have been avoided in order to make this book "reader friendly". Although this work is presented without footnotes, it is based on documentation. Any general reader interested in discovering primary and secondary background materials, notes, and sources should locate, without difficulty, the references in the detailed Bibliography. These references should also provide any knowledgeable scholar with the sources that substantiate the context.

The Bibliography lists the references drawn upon for the subject of this book but not its general background. The Bibliography therefore does not list every publication (book, pamphlet, essay, article, diary, letter etc.) and audio/video support that was utilized by the author relating to the subject's general topics.

It should be noted that the author attempted to touch upon, cover, or describe as many international entertainment styles, fields, areas, and trends as possible. However, in order to best relate the subject, the author chose to place special emphasis on the well-known popular categories. Also, the primary focus is on the entertainment industry within a North American context. To this end major sections have been dedicated to American and Canadian realities and business methods. The author felt most comfortable with this approach and regrets any specific type of entertainment business not adequately described. In addition, the author asks forgiveness for omitting any particular form of entertainment dear to the reader's heart. It is virtually impossible to mention, illustrate, or portray in detail the multitude of disciplines that contribute in different ways to the convergence of modern popular entertainment.

This book thus provides the reader with a general overview of the topics at hand. For example, it deals with the general principles found in the copyright laws of "treaty countries". A treaty country includes any Berne Convention country, any country adhering to any level of the Universal Copyright Convention, and any country member of the World Trade Organization. The United States, Canada, and most modern industrialized nations are considered "treaty countries".

This tome should increase the reader's awareness of the importance of intellectual property and the role it plays in modern society and show business. The basic concepts of copyright and trademarks are explained in relation to the work and creations of artists and manufacturers. For example, the author examines various aspects of American and Canadian copyright law and how foreign copyright laws and international copyright treaties affect North Americans. He also discusses digital copyright innovations and issues. This book provides answers to many copyright questions, and encourages the reader to ask more questions about this important area of the law. One should keep in mind, however, that no definitive answers yet exist from courts or legislators for many Internet and digital related copyright issues.

The reader should keep in mind that this book offers general intellectual property information only and does not cover all the complex issues that may arise through the copyright and trademark registration process. This tome is not a substitute for an experienced intellectual property lawyer, nor does it provide authoritative definitions and explanations, and decisions of boards, tribunals, and the courts. The material and content presented in this book is for informational purposes only. Its information is to be considered solely as a guide and should not be quoted as, or considered to be, a legal authority. Any opinions put forth should not be relied upon as, and do not constitute, legal advice. Authority must be found in the appropriate copyright and trademark laws and regulations, and in the decisions of the courts interpreting them. Legal information may become obsolete without notice. The reader is advised to consult a lawyer should legal advice be needed. If an attorney is hired, this book can certainly help the reader become a well-informed client.

Finally, this work does not do justice to all the important and often fascinating entertainment industry artists, pioneers, builders, entrepreneurs, innovators, technicians, and inventors who helped transform, deliver, and package entertainment into a commercial product, produced and marketed on a mass-commodity basis, and sold to a broad audience. The author, nevertheless, does wish to hereby salute them all. This popular industry would not have flourished without their talent, business acumen, labor, dedication, and accomplishments.

## POSTSCRIPT

The author wishes to pay homage to the many associations, organizations, and medical researchers dedicated to the understanding, educating, informing, researching, rehabilitating, and curing of hearing disorders. Entertainers, in particular, should better appreciate the miracle of hearing; it being one of the delicate human senses that must be protected and cherished. Please visit **www.markvinet.com** for links and information on this topic.

# PROLOGUE

*Writing is like painting or composing –*
*It's about the choices an author makes.*

There are numerous entertainment books that deal entirely and exclusively with one specific area, discipline, category or field of the entertainment industry. These works offer detailed in-depth studies and analysis of their chosen topic while I have chosen to present a general overview of the many facets of the entertainment industry. My primary goal is to expose the multi-faceted business of entertainment in one accessible tome. The entertainment industry is vast, complicated, and exciting with all sorts of entrepreneurial and career opportunities.

Generally speaking, entertainment that is enjoyed by the largest possible audiences is called popular entertainment. Modern popular entertainment is entertainment created as a commercial product of an industry devoted entirely to its manufacture and sale. Types of popular entertainment are numerous and should be divided into categories, fields, areas, or disciplines. Within each category, numerous subcategories may exist. Since its beginnings, modern entertainment has branched out into so many categories that no single description fits all of them with total accuracy. A few generalizations, however, can be made, keeping in mind that for all of them exceptions can be cited. There are many different types of entertainment. In some cases, the categories overlap or converge. Convergence is broadly defined as "the occurrence of two or more things coming together." For example, a fully integrated modern media company does business in many areas, including film, television, book publishing, and the Internet. While creativity is the spark that ignites the entertainment engine, convergence is the driving force behind modern entertainment.

The continuous advances in electronics and technology result in tremendous growth and opportunities. New techniques, such as the high-fidelity digital reproduction of sound/images and their widespread and rapid mass media dissemination throughout the world, allow entertainment works to dominate modern popular culture. Shaped by economic, social, and technological forces, popular entertainment is closely linked to the social identity of its artists, performers, and audiences. Although modern entertainment is sometimes thought to have meaning only for the time in which it was created, many works of entertainment have endured for decades and continue to have relevance and credibility.

The unending struggle between the propensity of the entertainment industry to centralize entertainment and the stylistic diversity of artists continues in the popular entertainment of the twenty-first century. North American entertainment may be viewed as a relationship between a mainstream nucleus and various marginal sectors outside the mainstream of the entertainment industry. Whereas the mainstream entertainment industry reproduces works, maintains a popular structure, and attempts to guarantee profits, those in the margins typically include independent companies and artists who provide creativity for new forms of entertainment, which are then sometimes absorbed into the nucleus and marketed to a broad audience. A prime example of this process can be witnessed in the mainstream success of video games. Initially a fringe form of entertainment, video games have since converged with the film and music industries into an important part of the worldwide entertainment universe.

American influenced popular entertainment is seen by some as an encroaching force upon the cultural identities of foreign nations, while others see it as a wonderful gift to the world. Historically, Canadian talent has made important contributions to American popular entertainment. Nonetheless, Canada has been striving to protect and develop its entertainment culture from this irrefutable American influence since the introduction in 1971 of legislation to create minimum levels of Canadian content in domestic media. This landmark policy is believed to have engendered a self-sustaining Canadian entertainment industry via the development of domestically produced popular entertainment. The juggernaut that is American entertainment creativity and influence cannot be underestimated and its impact is revealed in the pages you are about to turn.

I sincerely hope that this book will allow you, the reader, to better understand the mechanics of the entertainment industry, while facilitating the navigation of its sometimes tricky, treacherous, turbulent, but exciting waters.

A good book must be written by a good writer and read by a good reader; I've done my best … now it's your turn.

Enjoy the read,
Mark Vinet

# INTELLECTUAL PROPERTY
## COPYRIGHT
## TRADEMARK
## PATENT
## INDUSTRIAL DESIGN
## INTEGRATED CIRCUIT TOPOGRAPHY PROTECTION
## CONFIDENTIAL INFORMATION & TRADE SECRETS


*« Copyright protection is instantaneous and automatic »*


## CRITERIA FOR AUTOMATIC COPYRIGHT PROTECTION
### ORIGINALITY
### FIXATION
### NATIONALITY OF CREATOR or PLACE OF PUBLICATION


## COPYRIGHT PROTECTION METHODS
### GOVERNMENT CERTIFICATE OF REGISTRATION
### HOMEMADE DEPOSIT
### SPECIALIZED DEPOSITORIES


## ORIGINAL COPYRIGHT WORKS
### MUSICAL / ARTISTIC / LITERARY / DRAMATIC


## COPYRIGHT PROTECTS:
### ECONOMIC, NEIGHBORING & MORAL RIGHTS


## VIOLATIONS OF COPYRIGHT
### PLAGIARISM / CRIBBING / PIRACY
### BOOTLEGGING / COUNTERFEITING


## TYPES OF COPYRIGHT VIOLATION REMEDIES
### CIVIL / CRIMINAL / BORDER REMEDIES

# 1.  COPYRIGHT

Copyright is the principle source of power, control, and money in the entertainment industry. This fact must never be underestimated and should be properly understood.

Copyright means the "right to copy." Most copyright laws grant copyright holders the sole and exclusive right to perform, reproduce, or publish a work. These rights give copyright owners control over the use of their works, and an ability to benefit, monetarily and otherwise, from the exploitation of their creations. Copyright also protects the reputation of creators, and the rights of performers. Copyright law is considered part of a larger body of law called "intellectual property."

The word "intellectual" is used to distinguish it from "physical" property. Intellectual property law refers to and protects the intangible or intellectual nature of an object. Physical property law protects the tangible or physical aspect of an object. For example, the owner of a wooden table owns tangible, physical property while the owner of a song owns intangible, intellectual property. The former can actually be touched, while the latter cannot.

Some property possesses both a physical and intellectual property component, such as a book. The physical component of the book is the object itself, which can be held by a person's hands. The intellectual component of the book is the words that appear on the pages and the expression of any ideas contained in those words. The intellectual or physical components of any creation are separate. By owning the intellectual or physical property in a creation, you do not necessarily own the other kind of property in it. Therefore, owning a book does not mean that one owns the copyright in that book.

To better understand copyright, one must first look at the other various areas of intellectual property – trademark, patent, industrial design, integrated circuit topography protection, and confidential information & trade secrets. The registration of each type or category of intellectual property with a country's registration office usually requires paperwork and the payment of fees.

A trademark is a word, picture, symbol, design, logo, shaping of goods or combination of these, used to distinguish the services or wares of one person or organization from those of others in the marketplace.

A trademark proprietor has exclusive use of that mark to be identified with certain services or goods. Examples of trademarks are the word and logo "Coca Cola" and the distinctive shape of the Coke bottle. Trademarks are usually protected either by use, or registration for a specific amount of years, often renewable indefinitely for additional consecutive terms.

A patent is granted only for the physical embodiment of an idea, or for an innovative process that produces something commercial or tangible. New technology, communications systems, medicines, energy sources, and machinery are all patentable. However, you cannot patent an idea, a method of doing business, a medical treatment, a scientific principle, an abstract theorem, a computer program, nor any inventions having immoral or illicit goals or purposes. The patent legally protects a patent owner for a certain amount of years after an application for a patent is filed; allowing the owner to prevent others from using, making, and selling that invention within the country where the patent was obtained.

An industrial design is any original pattern, shape, or ornamentation applied to a useful article of manufacture. The utilitarian or functional features of that article are not protected by industrial design, but may be protected by a patent. It is the visually appealing or attractive part of the design, and not the article to which it is applied that is protected as an industrial design. The shapes of a chair, telephone, guitar, computer, or the decorations on a bowl are examples of industrial designs. Protection lasts for a specific amount of years, beginning on the date of registration of the design.

The newest kind of intellectual property protection is for the topography of integrated circuits. These integrated circuits or microchips, are tiny electronic devices found in everything from common appliances such as DVDs and dishwashers. Integrated circuit topography laws protect the original design of a registered topography on its own or when embodied in a product like a DVD. A topography is considered original if it is developed through the application of intellectual effort and is not the mere reproduction of a whole or substantial part of another topography. Registered integrated circuit topographies are usually protected for a specific amount of years from the date of filing the application for registration.

And finally, confidential information & trade secrets protect ideas, concepts, and factual information. For example, an idea for a book/movie/television show, machinery to build airplanes, or computer software may be considered confidential information. A client or customer list, or knowledge of a recipe for a certain spicy sauce or beverage, obtained by working at a fast food or soda pop company, may be considered trade secrets.

Unlike the other areas of intellectual property, confidential information and trade secrets are often not governed by statute, but are based upon common law. One of the best ways to protect trade secrets or confidential information is through written agreements. The more specific and limited the terms and conditions in the agreement, the more likely the contract will be upheld in a court of law.

North American copyright laws find their roots in old English laws and traditions. The history of American and Canadian copyright law originated with the introduction of the printing press to England in the late fifteenth century. As the number of presses grew, authorities sought to control the publication of books by granting printers a near monopoly on publishing in England. The *Licensing Act* of 1662 confirmed that monopoly and established a register of licensed books to be administered by the Stationers' Company, a group of printers with the authority to censor publications. The 1662 act lapsed in 1695 leading to a relaxation of government censorship, and in 1710 Parliament enacted the *Statute of Anne* to address the concerns of English printers and booksellers. The 1710 act established the principles of authors' ownership of copyright and a fixed term of protection of copyrighted materials (14 years, and renewable for 14 more if the author was alive upon expiration). The statute prevented a monopoly on the part of the booksellers and created a "public domain" for literature by limiting terms of copyright and by ensuring that once a work was purchased the copyright proprietor no longer had control over its use. While the statute did provide for an author's copyright, the benefit was minimal because in order to be paid for a work an author had to assign it to a bookseller or publisher. Since the *Statute of Anne*, North American laws have been revised to broaden the scope of copyright, to change the term of copyright protection, and to address new technologies. The United States first addressed copyright in its constitution of 1787. The First Congress implemented the copyright provision of the Constitution in 1790. The *Copyright Act of 1790, An Act for the Encouragement of Learning, by Securing the Copies of Maps, Charts, and Books to the Authors and Proprietors of Such Copies*, was modeled on the *Statute of Anne*. It granted American authors the right to print, re-print, or publish their work for a period of 14 years and to renew for another 14. The law was meant to provide an incentive to artists, scientists, and authors to create original works by providing creators with a monopoly. At the same time, the monopoly was limited in order to stimulate creativity and the advancement of "science and the useful arts" through wide public access to works in the "public domain." Major revisions to the act were implemented in 1831, 1870, 1909, and 1976.

Canada, like many other industrialized countries, first legislated its copyright laws during the early part of the twentieth century. The Canadian Copyright Act was first enacted in 1924 and, along with its annexes, schedules, rules, and amendments, has since governed copyright law in Canada. Canadian copyright law falls under federal jurisdiction and is consistent throughout the country.

The main goals of American and Canadian copyright laws, and copyright laws around the world, are basically the same. The underlying principles attempt to provide creators with adequate protection in their creations and provide users with reasonable access to these creations. When faced with differences between copyright laws, one should apply the international concept of "national treatment," for instance when using a work in the United States, American law should be applied. The United States and Canada generally protect the same types of works and grant similar rights to creators, though the terminology used in the respective legislation may differ.

Most copyright laws were introduced in an era before photocopying, VCRs (video cassette recorder), DVRs (digital video recorder), computers, and the Internet. However, most statutes remain flexible to meet the demands of today's technology, thanks in part to amendments made to them. Copyright evolution, update, and reform, is an on-going process.

Two concepts underlie and are vital to understanding how copyright laws work. A creator has two property rights in its creation. First, there is a right in the physical property, in the creation itself. Second, there is a right in the intangible property, attracting certain rights that govern the use of the creation. Copyright protects this second, intangible right. For instance, if you own a book, you may read it, display it in a bookcase and lend it to a neighbor. However, you may not do anything that only the copyright holder has the exclusive right to do, like reproducing, editing, or translating the book.

Copyright laws do not protect ideas. This concept is based on the notion that ideas are part of the public domain (not subject to copyright protection) and that no one can have a monopoly in them. Copyright laws protect the expression of ideas, rather than the ideas themselves. In practice, anyone can follow an idea set out in a pamphlet or an instructional audio/video disc, or create a work based on the same idea, without violating copyright. The concept also means that there can be copyright in two or more works expressing the same idea, since it is the original expression of the idea which is protected by copyright. For instance, two people may independently make drawings of the same cottage, each sketch being protected by copyright and neither of them violating the copyright of the other one.

In both the United States and Canada, copyright protection is instantaneous and automatic, existing upon the creation of a work or sound recording, or when a performance or broadcast signal occurs. However, there are three criteria for this automatic protection: originality; fixation; place of publication or nationality of creator. In order for material to be protected by copyright, it must be novel in the copyright sense of the word. A creation need not be completely original, nor does it have to possess some artistic, literary, or aesthetic quality to be protected by copyright law. Whether a creation is original in the copyright sense is always a factual question. In fact, the standard of originality is very low and one of degree, which ultimately a court must adjudicate. There are usually no definitions of "original" in copyright laws. North American courts, for example, have interpreted originality as possessing the following qualities: the work must originate with the author; the work must be the result of an independent, creative effort rather than a mechanical or automatic arrangement; the work must not be a copy of another work; the author must use skill, experience, labor, discretion, selection, judgment, taste, personal effort, ability, knowledge, reflection, and imagination. Works that may be protected by copyright include songs, print/electronic books, paintings, compilations, directories, statistical tables, dictionaries, translations, adaptations, as well as a novel arrangement of a public domain work.

In order for original work to be protected by copyright, it must also meet the criterion of "fixation." North American court cases have decided that copyright subsists only in works that are "expressed in some material form, capable of identification and having a more or less permanent endurance." This criterion reinforces the principle that copyright protects the "form" in which an idea is expressed and not the ideas contained within that form. For example, a fixed work can consist of a handwritten or typed manuscript on paper, or electronically saved on a computer or disc. Fixation of a musical work may be through concerts, by computer notation, or by a recording of the work on a laser disc, digital audiotape, analogue tape or film. Fixation of a choreographic work may be through sketches or by a recording of the work on video, even though these records are "interpretations" of the choreography and not the "work" itself.

Speeches, lectures, addresses, sermons, improvised theatre skits and musical jam sessions that have not been written down or recorded in some way prior to their presentation are examples of works that may not be considered fixed. An unsaved image or text on a computer screen may also not be considered fixed.

In order for material to be protected by copyright, it must also meet certain conditions concerning the nationality of the creator or the place of first publication of the work. In order to be eligible for copyright protection, the creator of any published or unpublished material must be a citizen or resident of a "treaty country" or the place of first publication of the work was a treaty country. A treaty country includes any Berne Convention country, any country adhering to any level of the Universal Copyright Convention, and any country member of the World Trade Organization. In addition, treaty governments can extend copyright protection to other countries where that country provides similar protections.

Authors and copyright owners are responsible for enforcing the rights set out under copyright laws. However, there are certain cases where the copyright laws provide "criminal remedies", and the government may institute an action against an alleged infringer of copyright.

Although copyright protection is immediate and automatic, registering, marking, and depositing a work may help enforce these rights. The copyright symbol ©, used to mark works protected by copyright, is a universal symbol of copyright notice. There are three elements to a copyright notice. The "c in a circle" or © (or the abbreviation "Copr." or the word "Copyright"), followed by the name of the copyright owner and the year of first publication. These elements should be included in the notice but need not appear in any set sequence. For example, the copyright notice for this book is © Wadem Publishing 2005. Although I am the author and original copyright owner of this book, I assigned my copyright to a corporation, which now is the legal copyright owner.

Using the © symbol is not mandatory under all copyright laws, however, there are certain advantages to marking a work. First, it is a reminder to the public that copyright exists in the work. As such, it provides evidence in a court action that the alleged infringer or violator should have known that copyright existed in the work. Second, it may help potential users find the copyright holder and obtain permission to use a work. Third, marking is beneficial if a court case is pursued in countries that preclude an alleged infringer from claiming that he/she did not know that copyright existed in a work, even though proper copyright notice was placed on it.

Copyright notice should be placed in a conspicuous way that gives reasonable notice of copyright, and in a location on a work that will not be missed by an observer. For example, copyright notice should always be included on the inside title page of a book, under drawings or photographs, on the actual laser discs that contain music or movies, and on the home page of a website.

Most government copyright offices provide a registration system for works protected by copyright. Advantages to voluntarily registering with the government are twofold: a certificate of registration creates a presumption that copyright is recognized in a work, and the name registered is the proprietor of the copyright in that work. Because this registration is usually voluntary and no deposit or formal filing of a copy of the work with the copyright office is required, some copyright owners voluntarily use additional registering or depositing methods to protect their works.

Mailing a copy to oneself (the method I choose to call "homemade deposit") is a longstanding, straightforward, and acceptable method that may provide additional proof in a court proceeding. A homemade deposit requires a creator to insert appropriate documents, manuscript, photographs of artwork/sculptures, music lead sheets, recordings, or any other reproduction of the work, in an appropriate envelope, box package, or container and mail it to oneself by registered mail. One should make sure the envelope is properly sealed and ask the post office clerk to stamp the package with that day's date. When the package is received, it should be stored with the registered mail slip in a safe place and not opened, unless and until one appears before a court of law. Once opened before a judge, the envelope and its contents will act as evidence in establishing a date of creation (the date of the post office stamp/seal will constitute a presumption of proof for the creation date), and ownership of copyright, in that protected material. Expect a possible challenge by opposing counsel as to the secure nature of the sealed package; thereby raising doubts that the materials found within may have been recently substituted.

In order to remove any doubt regarding the date of creation, I suggest the following foolproof method for homemade deposits. This new method is a variation of the traditional homemade deposit method described in the preceding paragraph. Prior to sealing materials in a container, include a visual recording showing the copyright owner displaying, singing, or reading the complete work in the presence of one or several very young and/or very old family members or friends. When opened before a judge months, years, or decades later, the persons filmed can testify as witnesses. Radical physical changes to their appearance (taller, heavier, older) or presentation of a death certificate in the case of absent witnesses, will help prove the date of the visual recording, homemade deposit, and creation date.

Once a creator has copyright protection in one country, automatic protection in other treaty nations is common. For example, once copyright protection in Canada exists, creators automatically have protection in the United States. As is the case in Canada, it is not mandatory to register copyright in the U.S. in order to have protection there. There are, however, benefits to registration in the United States. Unlike Canada, the United States Copyright Office requires that the owner deposit copies of the work when registering a copyright. This deposit may provide additional proof of copyright ownership. If a copyright infringement lawsuit is initiated in an American court, United States registration provides additional advantages in court proceedings. These advantages are especially important for copyright holders who exploit their works in the United States. Some Canadians register their works in the United States in order to benefit from the advantages of the American registration system.

Some artist unions, associations, and organizations have set up non-governmental systems to deal with the type of works they represent. These systems may provide evidence of proprietorship and proof of creation on a particular date, but they do not confer any copyright protection or give the owner the benefits of registering with a copyright office. Neither are there specific formalities or regulations governing specialized depositories. One must thus ensure that the chosen depository is legitimate and can guarantee that the work will be kept in safe storage for the necessary period of time. Examples of non-governmental services include those set up and administered by the Songwriters Association of Canada, the Writers Guild of Canada and the Writers Guild of America. These services will usually hold in deposit any draft and final recordings, scripts, treatments, and related materials for radio, films, television, videos and interactive media.

When considering copyright protection, unpublished works are the most vulnerable. Published works, by their nature, are usually available to the public as of their published date, thereby reinforcing copyright notice via an identifiable point in time when the work was widely, and perhaps even commercially, circulated. Unpublished works, on the other hand, usually remained low profile and somewhat anonymous.

The concept of international copyright protection does not formally exist. There is no one international copyright law, per se. Each country has its own copyright laws. However, one can have protection in other nations under that nation's copyright law through the copyright relations countries reciprocally share with each other. Generally, countries around the world have agreed to recognize and uphold each other's copyrights. There are two main international copyright conventions, the *Berne Convention for the Protection of Literary and Artistic Works* or the Bern Convention, and the *Universal Copyright Convention* or UCC. The United States and Canada are signatory to both of them. These conventions do not by themselves provide copyright protection. Their purpose is to provide minimum standards which member countries are required to include in their domestic copyright legislation and provide for "national treatment."

In copyright conventions, national treatment means that each country signatory to the convention must give nationals (citizens, landed immigrants or permanent residents) of other signatory countries at least the same copyright protection that it affords its own nationals. For example, an American author is entitled to the same copyright protection in Canada as any Canadian citizen (and vice-versa), by virtue of both countries being members of the Berne Convention.

The Berne Convention is the older, and more important, of the two international copyright conventions. It was concluded in 1886 and has been amended and updated many times. At present, there are approximately 150 member countries. The World Intellectual Property Organization or WIPO, an agency of the United Nations, administers the Berne Convention. The Berne Convention sets minimum standards of protection that signatory countries must include in their domestic law. These standards relate to the categories of material protected and the scope/duration of the protection. For instance, member nations must provide copyright protection for most kinds of material for at least the life of the creator and fifty years after the creator's death. In addition, members may only include exceptions to the exclusive rights of copyright proprietors that do not conflict with the normal exploitation of the material and do not unreasonably prejudice the legitimate interests of the creator. Once copyright protection is secured in one's own country, provided that it is a Berne Convention country, protection is immediate and automatic in all other countries that are also signatories to the Convention. Solely the laws of the country where protection is claimed govern the degree of protection and available remedies for violation of copyright.

Some countries did not quality and thus could not join the Berne Convention because their domestic laws did not conform to Berne standards, or because they had different legal systems. In response to this reality, a new, less demanding convention, the UCC, was adopted in 1952. Like Berne, the UCC sets minimum standards of protection that member nations are required to include in their domestic law. Unlike the Berne Convention, copyright protection is not immediate and automatic in UCC countries upon protection in one's own country. Creators from UCC countries are only protected on a national treatment basis in other UCC countries if they comply with certain conditions. One of the main conditions is that, from first publication, all copies of material published with the authority of the creator or other copyright owner bear the symbol ©, accompanied by the name of the copyright proprietor, and the year of first publication, placed in such manner and location as to give reasonable notice of claim of copyright.

Not all modern industrialized countries automatically sign international copyright conventions. It may sometimes take years before a country becomes a member. For example, Canada only became a member of the 1961 Rome Convention in 1998. The Rome Convention, or the *International Convention for the Protection of Performers, Producers of Phonograms and Broadcasting Organizations*, protects neighboring rights of performers, producers of sound recordings and broadcasters.

The Rome Convention sets out for performers and producers of sound recordings, a remuneration right when their recordings are either performed in public or broadcast in countries that have acceded to the Rome Convention.

In 1996, over 155 countries reached agreement on two new digital treaties, the *WIPO Copyright Treaty* or WCT and the *WIPO Performances and Phonograms Treaty* or WPPT. These treaties deal with copyright issues and needs in the digital era. Nations must have their laws in conformity with the treaties at the moment they adhere.

In the past, international copyright relations were only established through international copyright conventions and bilateral agreements. The United States and Canada, however, have signed international trade agreements that have provisions for intellectual property including copyright. These agreements include the *Canada United States Free Trade Agreement* or FTA, the *North American Free Trade Agreement* or NAFTA, and the agreement on *Trade Related Aspects of Intellectual Property Rights* or TRIPs, which is part of the Uruguay Round of the *General Agreement on Tariffs and Trade* or GATT. Countries that signed GATT are members of the World Trade Organization or WTO. These agreements are separate from the copyright conventions and are not intended to replace them. In fact, the trade agreements often require that nations provide as a minimum the protection required by the international copyright conventions.

Under the international system of copyright, copyright owners enforce their rights in the country where the alleged violation of copyright occurs. With the Internet, it is difficult to establish where violation of copyright takes place. Does it occur in the country where the work is uploaded onto a website, or where it is downloaded? Thus, a copyright infringement case may be initiated in the country where the copyright owner of the content resides, or where the alleged infringer resides, or possibly in another country if there is proof that the infringement took place in that other country.

Copyright protection subsists in original musical, artistic, literary, and dramatic work. A musical work is usually defined as any work of music or musical composition, with or without words, and includes any compilation thereof. A musical work, for copyright purposes, is a composition or song, but not a disc, digital audio or analogue tape or other object or media support that embodies the composition. Musical scores are protected by copyright. Original music is protected by copyright as soon as it is expressed and fixed in some permanent form. Examples of fixation include: sheet music or staff paper; saved on a computer hard drive or, laser disc or tape; or, printed out from a computer. Copyright protection may subsist in musical adaptation or arrangement provided it meets the general criteria for copyright protection including originality in the form of sufficient skill and labor.

Photographs, illustrations, paintings, maps, charts, drawings, sculptures, engravings, artistic craftsmanship and architectural works are examples of an artistic work. The test of an artistic work is whether the work is original, that is, whether it is an original expression of its creator and not copied from another source. An artistic work is generally not judged by its aesthetic or artistic nature.

A literary work protected by copyright includes all written documents, whether prepared in print or digital format. Generally, a literary work exists if the creator has used labor, skill, and ingenuity to arrange its thoughts. Accounting and scientific tables, letters, legal contracts, e-mails, computer programs, a lecture which is fixed in some form, and compilations of literary works are examples of literary works protected by copyright. Generally, government materials are also protected by copyright. This includes the works of federal, state, provincial, territorial and municipal governments.

In order for a work to be considered a dramatic work, there must be some dramatic action or performance. These dramatic elements need be fixed in some form in which the dramatic elements are recognized. A dramatic work includes a large variety of works such as any piece for recitation, mime or choreographic work, the scenic arrangement or acting form of which is fixed in writing or otherwise. Films, videos and any other cinematograph work, and any compilation of dramatic works are protected by copyright.

Important limitations do exist to copyright protection. For instance, copyright does not protect individual words, phrases, slogans and titles, although other forms of protection including trademark may be available. News has no copyright protection. However, as is the case with ideas and facts, once the news is put or fixed in some material form, copyright protection may apply to that particular expression of the news.

Copyright protection may apply to unprotected works, when compiled or collected in a specific way or if there is more than one author. A collective work is generally described as any work written in distinct parts by different authors, or in which works or parts of works of different authors are incorporated. Whether in print or in a digital form, examples of collective works include a dictionary, almanac, encyclopedia, anthology, yearbook, website, magazine or newspaper. In order to qualify as a collective work, there must be originality in the production of the work. Several copyrights may exist where there is a collective work. There is copyright in the collective work itself, and, there is copyright in each individual work included in the collection, provided that copyright already exists in those individual works and they are not in the public domain.

A compilation is a work resulting from the selection or arrangement of literary, musical, artistic, or dramatic works or parts thereof, or a work resulting from the arrangement or selection of information or data. A dictionary, encyclopedia, website, or computer disc may qualify as a compilation. A compilation is protected by copyright if certain elements went into the production of it, such as the compiler's original skill, knowledge, experience, research, time, labor, thought, judgment, arrangement, and selection in the making of the compilation. In order for a database to be protected by copyright, it has to meet the general criteria of compilations. For instance, there must be sufficient original skill, knowledge, judgment, and labor into the arrangement and selection of data. For example, telephone or zip/postal code listings are not considered databases, as the arrangement or selection of data only results in a protected compilation if the finished result qualifies as an original intellectual creation. In these cases, there is insufficient skill, knowledge, judgment, and labor involved in the overall arrangement of the compiled data to constitute an original intellectual creation protected by copyright.

A work of joint authorship is a work produced by the collaboration of two or more authors in which the contribution of one author is not distinct from the contribution of the other author or authors. Since there is only one work created when there are several authors of a work, there is only one copyright in a work of joint authorship. To be considered joint authors, each author must have contributed significant original expression to the work with the intention that their contribution be merged with that of the other author. Also, each author must have intended the other person to be a joint author of the work.

Copyright laws usually provide protection for non-traditional copyright materials. Broadcast or communication signals, an artist's performance, and audio recordings are examples of non-traditional copyright materials. These materials are protected on a different basis than works. Elements like originality and authorship do not apply to these non-traditional copyright materials.

A communications signal is generally defined as radio waves transmitted through space without any artificial guide, for reception by the public, such as a radio signal. Generally, protected broadcasts include television and pay-per-view broadcasts, but not satellite or cable retransmitted signals. For instance, a musical performer owns the copyright in his performance, the producer of a sound recording owns copyright in the recording, and a broadcaster who broadcasts a signal owns the copyright in the signal.

An artist's performance refers to live performances such as a musician playing a song, an orator reading a poem or story, or an actor acting in a play. It also includes a performance of a work in the public domain, or one that has not been recorded. Examples include an improvisation of a literary, dramatic, or musical work such as a jam session, and a recorded performance of an author, actor, dancer, singer, and musician on a variety of media including digital audio or analogue tape, laser discs, video, film, and compilations of these recordings.

A sound recording is a recording, fixed in any material form, consisting of sounds, whether or not of a performance of a work. Examples of sound recordings include a recording of music, lectures, seminars, dramatic recitals, and even a dog barking. Recordings of works that are in the public domain, such as a Mozart Concerto, may also be protected as a sound recording. Included, as well, are compilations of sound recordings on any sort of media support such as analogue tape, digital audiotape or disc, vinyl, and on the Internet. Three copyrights may exist when a sound recording is involved. There is copyright protection in the sound recording, in any protected works embodied on the sound recording, and in an artist's performance. Digitally sampling a copyrighted sound recording is a violation. Laws aimed at stopping piracy of recordings apply to digital sampling. For example, courts have ruled that rap artists should pay when they "lift" or "sample" another artists' work, even when sampling unidentifiable musical snippets – a note here, a chord there. Users are thus obliged to get a license or not sample. Courts do not see this restriction as stifling creativity in any significant way.

The creator or author of a work is the first proprietor of its copyright. This person created the work, or was the first person to express the idea in a tangible fixed form. A person who writes a book is its author and a person who designs graphics for a website page is the author of those graphics. The author of a letter owns copyright in that letter. Even after a letter has been mailed to someone else, the author of the letter retains the ownership of copyright in it. The same rules apply to all forms of electronic messages and e-mail.

The author of a photograph is the person who owns the initial film negative at the time when that negative was made. If there is no negative, the author is the proprietor of the initial digital photograph at the time when that photograph was made. The author is usually the first owner of copyright in the photograph. If the photograph, painted portrait, illustration or engraving is commissioned, the person ordering that work is the first proprietor of the copyright in it, provided the person ordering the work has offered and paid valuable consideration for the work, and the work was created because of the order.

Audio-visual works are subject to the general rule of ownership, but identifying the author and therefore first owner of copyright is not always clear. The author or first proprietor of copyright in a scripted audio-visual work is usually the maker of a cinematographic work, typically the person by whom the arrangements necessary for the making of the work are undertaken. The film's producer, director, or screenwriter may be considered its author. Often the producer is the owner, and the director is the author, of the work. The specific realities of each project may also help determine authorship; otherwise authorship should be clearly attributed beforehand in a written legal document between all parties concerned.

As is the case with scripted works, the author of a non-scripted work (improvised works, news coverage, home videos) is not always easily identifiable. Where a production company hires and is the employer of a producer and director, the company is the first owner of copyright in the non-scripted work. This does not, however, help determine who is the author of the work.

Copyright law is not always clear with respect to the ownership of musical works. Where one person creates the music and lyrics, that same person owns that song. However, where one author writes the lyrics and another composes the music, each contributor either owns copyright in their respective contribution or they jointly own copyright in the song as a whole. The author and first copyright owner of an adaptation or translation is the person who produces the adaptation or translation. The majority of copyrights in musical works are assigned to music publishers who then act on behalf of the authors of the musical works. Professional music publishers may be viewed as song-managers. They solicit commercial opportunities for the song and administer copyright and revenues. Most copyright permissions can be cleared through the music publisher.

Individual writers who make contributions to magazines, newspapers, or periodicals, are called freelancers. They are authors and first copyright owners of their work unless they have agreed otherwise. It is best to put in writing what uses may be made of a freelancers' contribution. For example, may the work be translated, edited, published in both print and electronic form, or sold to other publications?

Copyright exists in the collective work itself, and separately in each individual work in the collection. The person who selects or arranges the works in the collection is the creator and first proprietor of the copyright in the work as a whole. The individual copyright owners of these contributions continue to hold copyright in their contributions.

A compilation is an arrangement or selection of parts or wholes of copyright works or data, resulting in a new work like a database, encyclopedia or dictionary. The person responsible for making the compilation is the author and first copyright proprietor of that compilation. If copyright existed in any of the works in the compilation, the copyright holders of those works continue to own copyright in them.

When works are made in the course of employment, copyright ownership belongs to the employer where the creator of the work is an employee employed under a written or verbal contract of "service" or "work-made-for-hire". The work is created in the course of performing this contract and there is no provision in the contract that states that the employee owns the copyright. Independent contractors and consultants are the creators of, and own the copyright in, their works, unless they have agreed otherwise. The United States has different laws and industry standards than Canada for works created in the course of employment and for commissioned works. In employment or work-made-for-hire situations in the United States, the employer or other person for whom the work was produced is considered the author and proprietor of the copyright. This is true unless the parties have expressly agreed otherwise in writing. In Canada, even in employment situations, the original author of the work remains the author of the work for copyright purposes notwithstanding the fact that the employer is the owner of the copyright. This has important implications and consequences for such things as moral rights protection.

When works are made for or published by the government, copyright belongs to the government. This includes any work that is, or has been, prepared by or under the control or direction of any government department.

Corporations may be owners of copyright materials when dealing with commissioned/apprenticed/employed creators, or in the case where an author has assigned copyright to the corporation via a contract of service or work-made-for-hire. Corporations may also be authors, and thus owners, of copyright in sound recordings and photographs.

Generally, copyright in published works endures for fifty years after an author's death, until the calendar year end. This is known as the life-plus rule. Although life-plus-fifty is the minimum duration set out in the Berne Convention, the European Union countries and the United States protect copyright for at least life-plus-seventy. The general duration of copyright protection in Canada is for life-plus-fifty. Since the copyright law where the work is being used applies, Canadian works are protected in the United States for life-plus-seventy years whereas American works are protected in Canada for life-plus-fifty. The term of copyright is not determined by the life of the owner of copyright but instead by the life of the author, even where copyright has been transferred. Moral rights are also subject to the life-plus rule.

All copyright laws have exceptions to the life-plus rule; however, the rule generally applies to artistic, musical, literary, dramatic, choreographic, and audio-visual works, unless specifically provided for otherwise. Works that have not been published, made available to the public, performed in public or communicated to the public by telecommunication, fall into the category of unexploited works. The life-plus rule of duration applies to unexploited works.

In the case of collective works, the general life-plus rule applies in the collective work itself, as well as to each individual article in the collective work. If there are two copyrights in a collective work, one copyright may expire prior to the other one. Copyright duration in a joint work is usually based on the death of the last living author.

The life-plus rule applies to works prepared in the course of employment, and it is often based on the life of the author, and not the life of the employer or copyright proprietor. Materials prepared for and owned by the government have copyright protection for a minimum of fifty years to the calendar year end from the date of the first publication of the material. If the material is not published, then it is protected until publication plus a minimum of fifty years.

New material based on a work in the public domain may be a new copyright work. For example, an arrangement of a medieval folk song, an adaptation of a Beethoven Symphony or a translation of an Oscar Wilde play would acquire a new term of protection, based on the life-plus rule of the arranger, adapter or translator. For obvious reasons, works of unknown authors are dealt with differently. Copyright in anonymous and pseudonymous works usually lasts for the shorter of fifty years from first publication of the work, or seventy-five years from the creation of the work.

Some copyright statutes limit the life-plus rule via a reversionary interest proviso. Where the author of a work is also its first copyright owner, any copyright acquired by contract becomes void a specified limited period, for example twenty-five years, after the author's death. The copyright then becomes part of the author's estate. The proviso can be avoided if the creator disposes of the remainder of the copyright term by will. Where a work was not published, delivered, or performed in public prior to an author's death, the calculation for the specified limited period runs from the date of publication, delivery, or performance in public.

Copyright subsists in a sound recording for a minimum of fifty years from the calendar year end in which the first fixation of the sound recording occurred. Performances are protected for a minimum of fifty years until the calendar year end of its first fixation in a sound recording, or its performance if it is not fixed in a recording. Communication signals are protected for a minimum of fifty years after the end of the calendar year in which the signal is first broadcast.

Once copyright has expired in a work, the work is in the public domain. Public domain works are no longer protected by copyright and can be used freely, without obtaining permission from, or compensating, the copyright holder.

When dealing with copyright protected material, only a copyright owner may exercise, or authorize others to exercise, his rights. There are three kinds of rights set out in most copyright statutes: economic rights, neighboring rights, and moral rights. Copyright protects the economic interests of the authors and owners of musical, artistic, literary, and dramatic works. Moral rights protect the personality and integrity of an author of a work. Neighboring rights protect the economic rights of broadcasters, performers, and makers or producers of sound recordings.

A copyright holder has the exclusive right to reproduce a work or any substantial part of it in any material form. The right to perform a work in public gives the copyright owner the exclusive right to perform the work in public. The performance can be live or by means of the Internet, radio or television. However, anything less than a substantial part may be publicly performed without authorization. Also, the right to perform only refers to public performance. Thus, a recording may be played in your car or home, but not in a public place such as a restaurant or bar.

The right to publish a work means making copies of the work available to the public. Printing many copies of the work is not enough in itself; the copies must be made available to the public in order for publication to occur. The copyright owner has the exclusive right to initially publish a work, and to first make it available to the public. The copyright owner also has the right to translate, adapt and to telecommunicate a work to the public.

A copyright holder has the right to prohibit importation and prevent parallel imports of its work. Parallel imports refer to works that were legally published elsewhere but were imported without the consent of the rights holder. For example, a Canadian copyright owner has the right to ensure that pirated copies of its work are not imported into Canada, where the importer had knowledge that its activity violated copyright. Both authors and distributors can prevent parallel importation of protected works, or works represented through exclusive distribution arrangements.

Only the copyright owner may authorize the use of its sole and exclusive rights. If these rights are used without authorization or permission, then copyright is violated or infringed. For example, protected computer programs and musical works cannot be rented without permission from the rights holder. This rental right applies to the commercial rental of a sound recording of a musical work, and to certain computer programs.

Moral rights protect the personality, honor, or reputation of an author of a work. Since moral rights protect the author directly and are personal rights, they cannot be exercised except by creators themselves or by their heirs. These rights remain with the author even after copyright has been assigned in a work. Moral rights cannot be assigned or licensed, except upon the death of an author. However, creators may forfeit, waive or agree not to exercise in whole or in part their moral rights. Where an author waives his moral rights in favor of an assignee or licensee of copyright, any new copyright holder or licensee may also be privy to a previous waiver of moral rights unless the author has indicated clear restrictions against this. Clearing copyright does not mean that the moral rights in a work have been cleared. One must respect the moral rights of a creator unless the creator has waived those rights.

A key moral right is the right of paternity. A creator has the right, where reasonable in the circumstances, to be associated with the work as its author by name or under a pseudonym, and the right to remain anonymous. A second important moral right is the right of integrity. This is violated if the work is distorted, mutilated or otherwise modified, thereby causing prejudice to the reputation or honor of the author. Whether something is prejudicial in this manner is a question of fact that can be determined through evidence. For example, manipulating a recording, artwork, or digital photograph may be a violation, if the manipulation is prejudicial to the reputation or honor of the creator.

Another moral right is the right of association. A creator has the right to prevent the use of its protected work in association with a product, service, cause, or institution that is prejudicial to the reputation or honor of the creator. Once again, whether something is prejudicial in this manner is a question of fact. An example of this right might be the use of a song to promote the animal fur industry where the author's reputation rides on the fact of being a well-known anti-fur advocate.

Most copyright laws do not explicitly or specifically deal with such things as: the right to withdraw a work following its publication; or the right to revoke a license to use a copyright work where a licensed right has not been exercised; or the right to prevent the destruction of a copyright work – though this may be protected by other areas of law or established to be a modification which is prejudicial to the honor or reputation of an author.

Moral rights apply to digital works. The digital nature of these works, especially when available on the Internet, allows them to be easily appropriated, edited, modified, mutilated, distorted, and manipulated, thereby infringing moral rights.

The explicit moral rights protection that exists in the United

States only applies to those who create works of visual art. These artists have the right to claim authorship in their work, and to prevent the use of their name or identity in association with a work. In addition, the law grants artists the right to prevent the intentional mutilation, distortion, or other objectionable modification of certain works of recognized stature. Artists who qualify for federal moral rights protection can also prevent any destruction of certain works.

Copyright can be described as rights granted to authors of copyright works, whereas neighboring rights are rights granted to those who use these copyright works. Neighboring rights protect the rights of performers, record producers and broadcasters. For instance, copyright protects the author of a song and neighboring rights protect the performer of the song. The neighboring rights are rights in performers' performances, in sound recordings, and in broadcasts. The owner of neighboring rights may license or assign the rights in part or in whole.

Copyright laws usually impose certain specific limitations on rights. Certain provisions allow the use of copyright materials without the permission of, or compensation to, the copyright owner. In addition, there are several specific limitations or exceptions that apply to specific works or in specific circumstances. Certain conditions must be met to make use of these exceptions.

Fair dealing is a Canadian concept that provides a defense to someone who copies a small portion of copyrighted material. The courts have determined that the fair dealing defense is narrow and fact specific. Is a substantial part of the material being copied? This depends on the nature of the reproduction, and on the quantity and quality of the material used. There are no set rules, regulations, or percentages as to what qualifies as "substantial"; a court-of-law could find that reproducing a small percentage of a work is a "substantial part." If a substantial part is being copied, is the copying fair? Courts determine this based on numerous factors, including the quantity and quality of the copied portion, the competition between the infringing copy and the original material, and the availability of a license. For the dealing to be "fair", the use of the copied portion must be for one of the purposes set out in standard fair dealing provisions: private study, research, review, news reporting, or criticism. These purposes are interpreted narrowly. If a work is used for purposes of review, criticism, or news reporting, the source and the author's name must be mentioned. Fair dealing should not be confused with the American concept of "fair use," which allows for broader free uses without permission of the copyright owner. Therefore, Canadian works used in the United States may be subject to greater free uses than when the same works are used in Canada.

Generally, an owner of a legitimate copy of a computer program may make one back-up copy of that program without obtaining the copyright owner's permission, and may also modify or adapt that program for compatibility with a particular computer. Any copy must be destroyed as soon as the user ceases to be the owner of the original computer program. A copy may be made of a sound recording of a musical work, however in some countries, including Canada, home taping of television is not permitted, unless for educational purposes.

By and large, a drawing, painting, photograph, engraving or cinematographic work can be made (and published) of any sculpture or work of artistic craftsmanship if the work is permanently situated in a public location. The incidental inclusion of copyright protected material in other copyright protected material is permitted, for instance, where a news camera crew incidentally films a fashion show in which music is playing. Importation of protected works for personal use may be imported. New and used books may be imported for use by any non-profit museum/library/archive/educational institution, or for use by a federal, state, provincial or territorial government department.

Some materials can be used without the permission of the copyright owner for non-profit educational institutions (from pre-school to post-secondary education). The exceptions include: publication of written excerpts in collections for classroom use; reproduction for exam purposes; performances for or by students on school premises if the audience is primarily faculty, staff, and students; the use of a projector to project an image of a copy of a work; and taping of a television news program or other programs for educational and/or evaluation purposes. Some exceptions do not apply if the work, or a license from a collective society to reproduce the work, is reasonably available in the marketplace.

Most governments deal with copyright collectives and negotiate a blanket license for photocopying published print materials in all elementary and secondary schools. The license generally allows copying of up to ten percent of a book or an entire chapter (comprising less than twenty percent of a book), an entire newspaper article, magazine, or journal. In addition, post-secondary licenses cover limited photocopying by students, faculty and staff for school use, and in university libraries.

There are specific exceptions for non-profit public or research libraries, archives and museums. The exceptions allow these institutions to make a copy of a copyright work for the management or maintenance of its permanent collection. This mainly applies to preservation of documents and for internal records. They may also reproduce materials used solely for the purposes of private study or research. These non-profit institutions do not infringe copyright and are thus not liable for copying on photocopying machines if a copyright warning containing specified wording is posted in proximity to a photocopy machine on its premises and the institution has obtained a license from a copyright collective. Many of the exceptions, however, specifically exclude digital media or digital uses. For instance, an archive may not provide copies of a protected work in digital form although a photocopy of the same work may be provided.

Whether one owns the rights provided to copyright holders or wants to use them, these rights are exclusive and distinct. Each right is independent and separate from any other right, and the copyright holder has the exclusive right to do what he/she chooses with a work. As mentioned, the copyright is separate from the physical object in which copyright exists. Ownership of a physical object does not necessarily mean ownership of the copyright in the object. Further, moral rights and copyright are separate; an agreement dealing with one does not automatically deal with the other.

Only a proprietor of copyright or a person authorized by the owner may give permission to use a copyright work. Rights may be licensed or assigned. A license (i.e. lending) temporarily permits someone else to use a copyright work. A license may be exclusive or non-exclusive. Assigning rights means permanently transferring, selling, or giving copyright, either wholly or partially, to someone else. The new owner may use those acquired rights in the same manner as the former copyright holder did before the assignment, within the limitations of the contract setting out the assignment. An assignment is exclusive and cannot be granted to anyone else for the same term. Assignments in future works are common. For instance, a musician may sign a publishing agreement with a publisher for a yet unwritten song.

Copyright can be licensed or assigned in the following ways. A copyright holder may assign rights either wholly or partially. Thus, rights such as reproduction, publication, and performance in public can be licensed or assigned separately. Also, rights may be divided by time. A copyright owner may license or assign copyright for the whole term of copyright, or for any part of the duration of copyright. Further, rights may be divided by territory. For instance, a copyright holder may license or assign a right for a specific area such as the United States or Europe, or on a worldwide basis. Upon death, copyright can be passed on to other persons via testamentary dispositions specified in a will.

Obtaining permission to use a copyright work often means paying the copyright holder a pre-established set fee or by negotiating a fee to use the work. Copyright laws do not usually set out the remuneration or other compensation required for the use of a work. The value of a right or permission is generally a matter of negotiation. The price on assigning or licensing a copyright work is based on numerous factors including the nature of the copyright material, the demand in the marketplace, the popularity of the author, and how the material is to be used. As monetary compensation, the copyright owner may receive ongoing royalty payments based upon the quantity of copies sold or revenue received, or a one-time fee.

An assignment is usually only valid when it is in writing, signed by the copyright holder. Licenses may be granted orally, unless they are exclusive. However, a written contract is preferable as it can provide clarity and clearly set out the terms and provide proof of any agreement.

A collective society is an organization that administers the rights of several copyright owners. Collectives can grant permission to use their works and set the conditions for that use. Collectives are widespread, particularly for music performance rights, reprography rights and mechanical reproduction rights. Most collectives are affiliated with foreign societies; this allows them to represent foreign copyright owners as well. There are many copyright collectives, holder groups, licensing bodies, agencies, or societies that administer different rights on behalf of thousands of copyright holders. A copyright owner, therefore, need not exercise its copyright on an individual basis. For example, *BMI, ASCAP,* and *SOCAN* are three copyright collectives that manage the public performance of music on behalf of North American songwriters and publishers. A collective can negotiate comprehensive or blanket licenses that cover all of the materials that a collective society represents. Users pay in advance for use of the works during a specific time period. Alternatively, a collective can negotiate individual, transactional or specific use licenses. These licenses require clearance and payment each time material is used.

There are two types of copyright violations found in most copyright laws. Direct violation or infringement occurs where a protected right is directly violated. Indirect violation or infringement occurs through dealings with infringing copies, for example, the importation of unauthorized materials. Authorizing a person to reproduce a work without the permission of the copyright owner is also an infringement of copyright.

Copyright is violated by the exercise of any protected rights without the permission or consent of the copyright owner. It is irrelevant whether the protected work is marked as being protected by copyright, whether copying is done in good faith, whether the violator had any intention of profiting monetarily, or whether the violation was for non-commercial purposes. Ignorance of the law is no excuse.

There are several terms used to describe violations of copyright. Cribbing is the act of taking unauthorized intellectual material. Plagiarism is the act of appropriating the literary composition of another, or parts/passages or his/her writings, or the ideas/language of the same, and passing them off as the product of one's own mind. Plagiarism may violate the right to reproduce a copyright work and may also violate the moral rights of the creator. Where plagiarism is an appropriation of ideas, without the appropriation of the actual expression of those ideas, it is not a violation of copyright since copyright does not protect ideas.

Piracy is the illicit duplication of legitimate materials and is a violation of the right of reproduction and may also involve plagiarism. Bootlegging is the unauthorized recording of a live event like an oration or concert. It is a violation of the right in a performer's performance, and if copyright materials are being performed, a violation of the right in those underlying works. Counterfeiting is making a copy of something without authority and defrauding, misleading, or deceiving the public by passing that copy off as genuine or original. Counterfeiting involves a violation of the right of reproduction. Unauthorized copies may also be inferior reproductions of the original product thereby violating the author's moral rights.

Copyright owners are entitled to remedies for the violation of their rights. There are three general types of remedies found in most copyright statutes: civil, criminal and border remedies. A civil remedy allows a copyright owner to take legal action in certain civil courts against violators of its copyright. This includes anyone who allegedly uses a copyright work in a manner that only the copyright proprietor may use it, or any person who authorizes the infringing use of copyright material.

Multiple civil remedies are available to complainants or plaintiffs. An injunction is a court order, on behalf of a complainant, ordering an alleged violator to refrain from doing, or from continuing, a particular activity. Injunctions are costly but can be obtained rapidly. Injunctions can be awarded either at the start of a lawsuit or at the end of it. There are three main types of injunctions including: interim injunctions, granted for a short period of time, usually without notice to the offender, and before there is a judgment; interlocutory injunctions, continuation of an interim injunction; and permanent injunctions, granted at the end of a trial.

Once a legal suit is commenced, there is a danger that the alleged infringer disposes of illegal copies to eliminate evidence of infringement. Thus, a complainant may ask the court for an Anton Pillar order, which will order the alleged violator to allow the plaintiff or a representative to enter, inspect, and search the defendant's premises and seize any infringing copies or to take photos of them prior to any court proceeding. This pre-judgment request to the court is without warning to the defendant. An Anton Pillar order is very extreme and is only awarded under specific conditions.

Modern computer technology makes illicit on-demand publishing of textbooks a tempting business model. Similar to the music industry's response to peer-to-peer websites and the illicit copying of music, the book publishing industry is committed to stopping illegal copying activities in print or electronic forms wherever they occur. For example, courts have prevented copy-shops from making illegal copies of whole textbooks and selling them to students at dramatically reduced prices. Courts will often grant plaintiffs an Anton Pillar order enabling them to seize unauthorized copies of textbooks and other materials if the violating company is still in the business of making and selling such works.

Damages are monetary compensation recovered in a judicial proceeding by a complainant whose copyright has been violated. A court may award damages to a complainant even if the violator made no profit. A copyright holder whose works are not licensed by an appropriate collective, but are eligible to be, is limited to the amount of royalties it would have received if it were an affiliate of such a collective.

Statutory damages allow a copyright owner to collect specified damages as set out in copyright statutes, as opposed to actual damages resulting from the violating activities. A copyright holder may request at any time before a final judgment in a court case, in lieu of damages and profits, statutory damages in respect of each infringed work. A court may choose to award such part of the profits that the violator has made from the infringement as the court may decide to be just and proper. This account of profits can be awarded in addition to regular damages. A copyright infringer must give or delivery up to the complainant all infringing copies of a work, and all materials used to produce the infringing copies.

Copyright statutes usually set out two presumptions: that copyright subsists in a work, and that the creator of the work is the proprietor of copyright in that work. A defendant who wishes to prove otherwise has the burden of proof of doing so. Once the existence of copyright and proper ownership of the work is established, the plaintiff must prove that an infringement occurred. Once the plaintiff has presented the case, the defendant has an opportunity to prove that he has not violated copyright.

Where the extent of the infringement makes it too costly for an individual to take legal action, or where the illegal conduct should be set as an example to discourage others from engaging in the same or similar activities, criminal remedies may be more appropriate than civil sanctions. With criminal sanctions, a copyright holder must file a complaint with the police. It is then up to the police to investigate the alleged criminal offence. It is important to note that a criminal proceeding does not preclude a civil proceeding.

Border remedies permit customs officers to detain suspected infringing materials at a country's international border. To obtain such a remedy, a court must be satisfied that the material, to the knowledge of the importer, would have infringed copyright if made by the importer.

As explained, only a copyright owner, or authorized representative, can give permission to use copyright protected material. Finding the holder of a copyright work is not always easy. In the case of a published work, one should contact the publisher, producer, distributor, or retailer to help identify the copyright holder. One should also attempt to contact associations, organizations, unions, guilds, or collectives that might have knowledge of the copyright holder. Most treaty countries have many copyright collectives for different types of works and for specific rights. Often, these collectives have relationships with collectives in other treaty countries. Obtaining permissions from collectives is cost efficient and time effective. Another option is to search the appropriate national government copyright registers. Finally, the Internet may also be a helpful tool in locating a copyright holder.

If a copyright owner cannot be located, one may apply for a non-locatable copyright owner license. Before this type of license is granted, sufficient proof must be presented to the appropriate licensing body that every reasonable effort was made to locate the copyright owner.

Not all government materials require government permission to reproduce, adapt or translate, in whole or in part, or to use in any other copyright manner. It is often legal to reproduce certain government materials without charge or permission, if due diligence is exercised in ensuring the accuracy of the materials reproduced and the reproduction is not represented as an officially sanctioned version.

In general, the principles and laws of copyright applicable to traditional media are the same as those applicable to works in digital formats. The rights of public performance, adaptation, the right of telecommunication to the public, and the right of exhibition applies to digital works. The rights in performers' sound recordings, performances, and broadcast signals apply to digital recordings, public performances, and broadcasts. The existing rights in most copyright statutes apply to digital media. The right of reproduction includes digital reproductions, such as: an electronic book, image or photograph; a digital audio and/or video recording; and a compilation of works such as a CD ROM anthology or a website. Works protected also include online material if it is fixed in some form, for instance, as a print out, or if it is saved on a disk, hard drive or other back-up mechanism. Some content on websites may be reproduced without permission, for example, if the content is in the public domain, or if there is a copyright notice posted on the website allowing certain uses.

Licensing electronic rights and compensation for digital rights is a matter of negotiation between the contracting parties. Some copyright collectives offer digital licenses in specific circumstances for digital uses of published works. In establishing a value for such rights, the influence of future technological advances should always be considered. Technology is incessantly redefining the meaning of copyright in general, and of electronic rights and digital copyright in particular. New and effective copyright laws, revisions, and amendments must continuously deal with the past, as well as the future.

# COPYRIGHT TRUTHS

*Ignorance of the law is no excuse for copyright infringement.*

*Copyright does not protect individual words/phrases/slogans/titles.*

*Copyright laws do not protect ideas,*
*Copyright laws protect the original expression of ideas.*

*"Originality" in copyright possesses the following qualities:*
*the work must originate with the author;*
*the work must be the fruit of an independent, creative effort rather*
*than a mechanical or automatic arrangement;*
*the work must not be a copy of another work;*
*author's use of skill, experience, labor, discretion, selection, taste,*
*imagination, judgment, effort, ability, knowledge, reflection.*

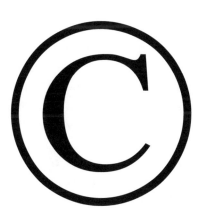

# 2.  TRADEMARKS

Success in the competitive global entertainment marketplace depends in part on the reputation of the product or service offered, as well as the message and the image conveyed and projected. A strategically strong presence and identity in a fast-paced world is vital. The public usually gravitates towards familiar names and symbols that have become associated with reliability and quality. That's why artists and entertainment companies spend millions of dollars developing and nurturing their images. They may research, design, market, and protect a logo, name, or package design as much as the physical product itself.

A significant way of protecting artistic, business or corporate identities is through a registered trademark. Registration of a trademark is legal title to intellectual property in much the same way as a deed is title to a piece of real estate. With a basic knowledge of the trademark concept and process, appropriate steps can be taken to protect intellectual property and avoid infringing the rights of others, thus avoiding time-consuming and costly legal battles.

In most countries, government agencies are responsible for registering trademarks. The main functions of these trademarks agencies/offices are to: receive and examine applications for trademark registration and grant registrations to qualifying applicants; record and index trademarks; approve and record assignments of trademarks; maintain an electronic inventory of trademark registrations and pending marks; provide a search room of these records for public use; provide general information to the public about the trademark registration process; publish trademark journals; and, maintain a list of trademark agents.

A trademark is a word, picture, symbol, design, logo, shaping of goods or combination of these, used to distinguish the services or wares of one person or organization from those of others in the marketplace. Trademarks come to represent not only actual services and wares, but also the reputation of the producer. As such, they are considered valuable intellectual property. A registered trademark can be protected through legal proceedings from imitation and misuse.

There are three basic categories of trademarks: ordinary marks, certification marks and distinguishing guise. Ordinary marks are words, symbols, or a combination of these features that distinguish the services or wares of a specific individual or firm. For example, a jazz music ensemble called "Sapphire" could register the word as a trademark for the services offered, assuming all legal requirements were met.

Certification marks identify services or wares that meet a defined standard. They are owned by one organization (often non-profit) but licensed to others to identify services or wares that meet a defined standard. Examples are: the logo of the Quebec Bar Association used by its lawyer members; the 100% PURE FLORIDA logo used on orange juice cartons; and, the word "Champagne" used only by sparkling winemakers of a specific region of France.

Distinguishing guise identifies the shaping of wares or their containers, or is a mode or style of packaging or wrapping wares. One of the best-known examples of this type of registered trademark is the distinctive shape and distinguishing guise of the Coke bottle.

A trade name is the name under which an artist or business, whether it be one's own name, or the name of a company or a partnership or a name adopted for a division of that business. The trade name can be registered under trademark statutes only if it is also used as a trademark, that is, used to identify wares or services. For example, let's say someone owns a movie theater and their corporation is called Screens Inc. People know their movie theatre under the name "Screens," because they use it as a trademark on or in association with their movie theater. They can, therefore, register Screens as a trademark. However, if people know the movie theatre under another word promoted by the company, for example "Flixs," then even though the official name of the company is Screens Inc., no one associates it with its wares. Therefore, Screens cannot be considered a trademark unless the company begins to use it as one.

In certain circumstances, a trademark registration in one country may be declared invalid because of the prior use, in that country, of a trade name that is similar to the registered mark. One should conduct a search of existing trade names before filing a trademark application. To ensure a thorough search, a recognized trademark agent or attorney should be hired to do the work.

A registered trademark is one that is entered on an official government trademark register. Registration helps solidify clear rights to the trademark. Registration may be cancelled if the owner fails to use the mark for an extended period. Although it is highly recommended, in most cases registration is not required. Using a mark for a certain period of time can establish ownership through Common Law – known as a Common Law trademark. Use of an unregistered trademark can lead to lengthy, costly legal disputes over ownership and the right to use it. Registration, on the other hand, is prima facie evidence of ownership. In a legal dispute, the registered proprietor does not have to prove ownership; the burden of proof is on the challenger.

Registration of a trademark in one country gives the owner of that mark exclusive right to use the mark throughout that country for a specific length of time, with options of renewal thereafter. A registered trademark is a valuable asset for business expansion through licensing franchises. To apply for a trademark in other countries, the owner must apply for registration directly to the countries in which it seeks registration.

In most countries, users can prepare and file trademark applications on their own, however, preparing an application and following through on it can be a complicated endeavor, particularly if a third party challenges the applicant's right to the mark. To ensure quality results, hire an experienced, competent trademark agent or attorney to do the job.

Individuals, partnerships, companies, trade unions, and lawful organizations and associations may obtain registration of their marks of identification for services or wares, provided they meet the legal requirements and pay the various registration fees; these costs do not take into account the fees of an agent or attorney. Once filed, applications then go through a rigorous examination process to make sure that they meet all requirements. In most cases the mark must be used before it can be registered. While the application may be based on proposed use, the applicant must put the mark into use before registration can occur.

When a trademarks office receives an application, it proceeds with a multi-step examination process. Firstly, it searches the trademarks records to find any other trademark that may come into conflict with the one submitted and, if one is found, informs the applicant. Then it examines the application for compliance with the requirements of the appropriate statutes and regulations, and informs the applicant of requirements that are not met by the application. The next step involves the public notice or publication of the application in the trademarks office's weekly trademarks journal. Time is allowed for challenges or opposition to the application. Anyone may, upon payment of a government fee, file a statement of opposition. After considering the evidence filed by either or both parties, the trademarks office decides whether to refuse the application or reject the opposition. The parties are duly notified of the decision with detailed explanations. If no one files an opposition to the application, the mark is allowed. Upon payment of the registration fee and the filing of a declaration of use in the case of a proposed use trademark application, the mark is registered.

The registration is valid for a set number of years, with the option to renew the registration prior to the expiration date. Fifteen year renewable periods are typical terms. Registering a trademark in one country protects the mark in that particular country only. If wares or services are offered and sold in other countries, foreign registration in each of those countries should be considered.

Various restrictions prevent certain marks from qualifying for registration. For example, a trademark will not be registered if the mark is primarily a person's full name or surname. An exception to this rule is allowed if it can be proven that the wares or services have become known under a person's full name or surname, so that the word now connotes more than a person's name or surname in the public's mind. There are many examples of personal names that have become associated with products and are now registered trademarks, for instance McDonald's restaurants. Another exception is if the name is a recognizable word or has meaning other than just as a name, for instance Green. This word could be registered for a trucking business as long as there were no other reasons to disqualify it.

A word that clearly describes a feature of the wares or services cannot be registered. For example, "tasty" for chocolate, "fresh" for vegetables, and "quick" for delivery services could not become registered trademarks. All fresh vegetables can be described as "fresh" and all chocolate as "tasty"; these are inherent characteristics of the wares. If permission were given to register these words, no other vegetables sellers or chocolate vendors could use them to promote their goods, which would be unfair. However, if you can establish that "Tasty Chocolate" has become so well known that people automatically and exclusively think of the applicant's product when they hear the words, trademark may be possible.

A further restriction is if the mark is not clearly descriptive, but clearly misleading or deceptively descriptive. For example, it is not possible to register "pure" for an artificially flavored beverage, and "fine dining" for a fast food restaurant.

An applicant may use clearly descriptive words, not registrable on their own, in a trademark with the understanding that no rights shall be claimed over them. A disclaimer is a statement indicating that the applicant does not claim exclusive rights for a certain word or words appearing in the trademark. For example, the trademark Prelude Music Store (used as a trademark for the operation of a record store) would require a disclaimer of the words "Music Store" as these are words that are clearly descriptive of the character of the services and should therefore remain available for all to use within this field. A typical disclaimer statement would read as follows: "The applicant disclaims the right to the exclusive use of the words Music Store apart from the trademark as a whole." Therefore, these words are still part of the trademark, but the applicant is not claiming exclusive rights for these specific words.

Registration will usually be invalid for a word that clearly designates the place of origin of the services or wares, or that misleads the public into thinking that the wares come from a certain place if they do not. Thus, Vermont Maple Syrup, Russian Vodka, Montreal Travel Agency, New York City Theater, or French Perfume could not be registered for those particular wares and services. Allowing the use of place names as part of a trademark would amount to giving a monopoly on a geographical term and be unfair to others.

Words that constitute the name of the services or wares in another language are prohibited and cannot be registered, for example "livre," French for book or "fiesta," Spanish for festival.

Words that suggest another trademark should be avoided. Confusingly similar words to a registered trademark or a pending mark will be refused. This prohibition makes sense when you recall that the whole point of registering a trademark is to protect business identities from confusion or imitation with others. Trademark examiners take into account various factors when determining whether trademarks are confusing or imitations. For instance, they determine: whether the trademarks sound or look alike and whether they suggest similar ideas; and whether they are employed to market similar services or wares.

Examples of confusing trademarks would be: "Spy Guitars" vs. "Spy Accordions" – two companies, two different product lines, but the same trademark and the same general area – musical instruments. However, "Spy" for watches could probably co-exist as a registered trademark with "Spy Guard" as a registered trademark for security services, because the services and wares in this example are very different.

Trademark statutes sometime expressly prohibit other kinds of marks. These prohibitions are designed to prevent applicants from misleading the public and unjustly benefiting from the prestige and authority of well-known and respected institutions. For instance, it is not possible to register a trademark that resembles certain official symbols unless consent of the authority in question is obtained. These official symbols include: official government symbols and flags; royal family or aristocratic coats of arms; badges and crests of military forces; emblems and names of international organizations like CARE, the Red Cross, and the United Nations; armorial bearings, symbols, and flags of other countries; and symbols of states, provinces, municipalities and public institutions.

Another prohibition covers the use of signatures or portraits of living persons or persons who have died within a certain amount of years (the preceding 30 years is a common amount of time). For instance, using the photo of a famous actor to promote a DVD retail store would be prohibited unless formal consent to do so was obtained from the actor or the actor's estate. Most trademark laws also prohibit subject matter that is immoral, obscene, or scandalous. For instance, a trademark may not include obscene visuals, profane language or ethnic slurs.

Trademarks offices maintain a public electronic inventory of all registered trademarks and pending applications. Before applying for trademark registration, it is a good idea to conduct a thorough preliminary search of the electronic registers and the trademarks database to see if the mark in question could be confused with another. While not mandatory, pre-screening will help determine whether the application has a chance for success, or whether it would be a waste of time, effort, and resources to try to register it in its present form. The applicant might, at this stage, want to consider modifying the trademark to add or adopt more original words or artwork. A preliminary search can also help avoid trademark infringement and potential lawsuits.

Electronic trademarks inventory contain listings of pending and registered applications. The electronic indices cover word marks, numbers, pictures, slogans and combinations of these. As soon as a new application is received, it too becomes part of the public record and is subject to inspection by the public. To conduct a proper search, various possible versions of the mark should be checked. In the case of a word mark, you should look for all conceivable spellings. Also, most office records contain samples of badges, crests, and official symbols that fall into the prohibited marks category. These samples can help an applicant determine if its mark does not fall into a prohibited category.

Trademarks offices usually do not conduct the searches, or advise on whether the applying mark is registrable. The registrable status of the trademark will be determined in the examination process of the trademark application. The applicant should also conduct a preliminary search of trade names. Trade names are often also used as trademarks, even if they are not registered as such. Users of trade names can thus argue ownership of the word as a trade name, as well as a trademark. As trade names may be recorded separately in each state or province, there are usually no complete central inventories containing all current names. This search is therefore quite complicated and time consuming, but could potentially help prevent unwanted problems.

Generally, trademarks offices in most countries follow similar registration procedures, however, specific steps and application fees do vary. Most countries require foreign applicants to appoint a native representative to whom the trademarks office correspondence will be directed.

The principal document in the registration process is the application form. Separate applications are filed for each trademark, although one application may cover both services and wares or a number of services or wares. If the trademark is anything other than a word or words in lower or upper case letters, then a drawing of the design is required at the time the application is filed. The formal drawing should be in black and white, and include a description of the colors, if colors are claimed in the trademark. Including color, however, allows for less flexibility, requiring that the trademark always appear in those specified colors. If the design is simply presented in black and white, the owner will be free to use the mark in any color. Likewise, presenting a word mark in any style of lettering other than lower or upper case imposes restrictions. For maximum flexibility, the word mark should be presented in lower or upper case and the design in black and white.

When an application arrives at a typical trademarks office, the staff will verify it to make certain it is complete. If anything is missing, they will contact the applicant and ask for information or documents. Once this process is finished, the office acknowledges receipt of a completed application and assigns a filing date – the date that the application is officially filed. This date should not be confused with the registration date. This filing date is particularly important for proposed use trademark applications; since it is the date most trademark statutes deem to be the entitlement date of a trademark application. After the formal filing, minor changes to the application are usually permitted. Major modifications, however, would entail the trouble and expense of another filing. To avoid this, diligence in preparing the application is preferable.

Trademarks office personnel conduct a thorough search of the official records to verify that the submitted trademark cannot be mistaken for another. They also conduct research to determine whether the applicant's mark fulfils all the criteria of the applicable trademark statutes, ensuring that it does not fall into any of the categories described hereinabove. The results are then carefully reviewed and considered by an assigned trademarks examiner.

The examiner studies the data and decides whether the application can be accepted. If there are doubts, the examiner will notify the applicant of the objections in writing, giving the applicant an opportunity to respond. If the answers still fail to satisfy the examiner, the applicant will receive a letter informing that the application has been refused and explaining the reasons why. In the event of refusal, an applicant usually has the right to appeal to a court of review. The examiner may request that the applicant disclaim the right to the exclusive use, apart from the trademark, of a portion of the trademark if the appropriate disclaimer statement has not already been included in the application.

If an applicant fails to take all the steps necessary to complete the process, its application may be considered abandoned. Before this happens, the applicant will be notified and given an opportunity to remedy the situation within a specified time period. If the applicant does not respond appropriately, its application will be considered abandoned and the applicant will have to re-apply with the requisite fees to pursue the trademark.

A second pre-publication search is then conducted to ensure that in the intervening months since depositing the application, no one has registered or applied for registration of a conflicting trademark. If the pre-publication verification has not brought to light any new objections the application is ready for advertisement in the official trademarks journal. This journal contains details about every application that has been approved for advertisement. When an application is advertised, it allows the public an opportunity to raise objections to pending applications prior to registration. It is another means of eliminating trademarks that conflict with those of other owners. The journal entry for the applicant's mark is a summary of the information on the trademark.

Any party with valid grounds for doing so may oppose a trademark application advertised in the journal. An opposition must be made within a limited timeframe of the publication date by either filing a statement of opposition and fee or by requesting an extension of time to oppose with a fee. The trademark office will dismiss an opposition it considers to be frivolous and unsubstantiated.

Opposition is a complex adversarial process that can absorb much time, effort, money and resources. Opposition proceedings are conducted much like court proceedings, during which both parties may file evidence and counter-arguments, cross-examine the evidence of the other party and make representations at an oral hearing. The whole procedure can take years. After a final decision is rendered, it may be appealed to an appropriate court of appeals. If there is no opposition, or if an opposition has been decided in the applicant's favor, the application will be allowed. The trademarks office will not consider any further challenges. The applicant will receive a notice of allowance and be asked to pay the registration fee. If the application has been based on proposed use, the applicant will be asked for a declaration stating commenced use of the trademark. The final step requires the office to issue a certificate of registration and enter the registration on its records.

The registration of a trademark provides the registered owner with an extremely valuable right, namely, the exclusive right to the use the trademark in respect of the registered services and/or wares, throughout a specific country. However, in order to maintain such a right, the registered owner must fulfill some requirements and responsibilities. One responsibility is that the registered owner pays a renewal fee every term; fifteen-year terms are common in many countries. Failure to pay such a fee on time will result in the cancellation of the trademark registration. Another responsibility of the owner is to use the trademark in the country that registered the trademark. If the trademark is not in use, then the registration is liable to be expunged by the appropriate authorities or court. The whole procedure can take a few years with all parties given the chance to argue their case. After a final decision is rendered to expunge, amend or maintain the registration, it may be appealed to a higher court.

A trademark is a form of property. An owner can therefore sell, bequeath or otherwise transfer its rights to another party through a transaction called an assignment. Trademarks offices should be immediately and formally notified of any such changes in ownership so that the office can amend its records accordingly.

Not all trademarks statutes contain mandatory marking requirements. Nonetheless, trademark owners usually indicate their registration through certain symbols, namely, TM (trademark), SM (service mark), R (registered) in a circle ®, MD (marque déposée) or MC (marque de commerce). The symbols TM, SM or MC may be used regardless of whether the trademark is registered. The R in a circle, or MD, on the other hand, should be used only if the mark is registered. Trademark notice should be placed in a conspicuous way that gives reasonable notice of trademark, and in a location that will not be missed by an observer.

Even though a country's laws may not require the use of these symbols, it is advisable to use them because there are certain advantages to marking trademarks. First, it is a reminder to the public that trademark exists. As such, it provides evidence in a court action that the alleged violator should have known that trademark existed. Second, it may help people locate the trademark owner and obtain permission to use it. Third, marking is beneficial if a court case is pursued in countries that preclude an alleged violator from claiming that it did not know that trademark existed, even though proper trademark notice was clearly visible.

One of the functions of trademarks offices is to prevent anyone from registering a mark that is the same as or confusingly similar to a registered mark. It does not, however, keep an eye out or actively search for cases of infringement. It is entirely the owner's responsibility to monitor the marketplace and, if a party is found using its registered trademark or a mark or a trade name that is confusing with its mark, to take legal action. A party that infringes on trademark rights may be accountable to the owner by way of an injunction, thereby ordering the infringer to cease the infringing activity and/or pay damages.

Preventing imitation by competitors is not the only reason to police your mark. If a business is a big success, its trademark may be in danger of becoming a generic term. For example, if the general public starts saying "Screeners" when they mean any movie theatre, that trademark may no longer be distinguishable from others. Such was the fate of trademarks like "Zipper, " and "Escalator" – the correct terms are "slide fastener" and "moving staircase". Too much familiarity can be a negative thing. This is why some owners are extremely vigilant about policing their marks, and preventing improper use of their trademarks in any kind of communication.

# A **TRADEMARK** IS USED TO DISTINGUISH THE SERVICES AND/OR WARES OF ONE PERSON OR ORGANIZATION FROM THOSE OF OTHERS IN THE MARKETPLACE.

## TRADEMARKS

**WORD**
**PICTURE**
**SYMBOL**
**DESIGN**
**LOGO**
**SHAPING OF GOODS**

## TRADEMARK OWNERSHIP SYMBOLS

**TM (trademark) ™**
**SM (service mark)**
**R (registered) ®**
**MD (marque déposée)**
**MC (marque de commerce)**

# *ENTERTAINMENT INDUSTRY TRUTHS*

**ARTISTS INITIALLY OWN 100% OF THEIR TALENT, COPYRIGHTS, TRADEMARKS, AND REVENUE POTENTIAL**

———————

**BUILDING AN ARTISTIC CAREER IS LIKE BUILDING A HOUSE, YOU CAN EITHER BUILD ON YOUR OWN OR BUILD WITH THE HELP OF OTHERS**

———————

**NEGOTIATING IS LIKE DATING, GET TO KNOW YOUR PARTNER BEFORE TYING THE KNOT**

———————

**TRUST BUT VERIFY**

———————

**IT IS BETTER TO OWN 50% OF SOMETHING, THAN 100% OF NOTHING**

———————

**WRITE THE CONTRACT = CONTROL THE NEGOTIATION**

———————

**MAKING $$$ AND GETTING PAID ARE TWO DIFFERENT THINGS**

———————

**DOUBT WHAT YOU HEAR, TRUST WHAT YOU SEE**

———————

**NEVER BE IN A RUSH TO FAIL**

———————

**SOMETIMES THE BEST DEAL IS NO DEAL**

# 3. ENTERTAINMENT DEALS & CONTRACTS

Entertainment contracts are voluntary agreements between two or more persons that create obligations to do or not to do a particular thing. Simply put, a contract is a promise that is enforceable by law. Generally, a promise is enforceable only if it is made in exchange for consideration, that is, a payment or something of value, for some action, or for another promise. A contract thus exists when an offer is made and then accepted. For a contract to be valid, both parties must indicate that they agree to its terms. All contracts must be entered into both willingly and freely, and an offer generally cannot be rejected once it has been accepted. Only those terms expressed in the contract can be enforced; hidden or secret intentions are not recognized. For a contract to be binding, it must not have a criminal or an immoral purpose or be against public policy. Since a contract is an agreement, it may be made only by parties with the capacity to reach an understanding. Both parties must have the competence to understand the terms of the contract they are entering into, and the consequences of the promises they make. Therefore, infants, individuals suffering from severe mental illness, or persons under influence of drugs or alcohol are unable to make binding contracts. A contract must also be the voluntary agreement of the parties; thus, it is void if it is procured by coercion, duress or fraud. Fraud may constitute misrepresentation by one party of the facts inducing one of the parties to enter the contract. A contract can be unenforceable if the terms are unreasonably favorable to one party. When agreements are so one-sided as to be found unconscionable, they are sometimes considered unenforceable contracts of adhesion.

The entertainment industry generally operates on the basis of short-term contracts. Entertainers perform a service as described in a contract and those with whom the agreement was made pay them for that service. Long-term exclusive personal services contracts, however, constitute an important part of the music industry. For example, music recording contacts can last for years. Entertainment enterprises usually offer the rights to commercialize their wares for a set period or term; however, the permanent sale, transfer or assignment of rights/services/products is also accomplished via contracts.

The essentials of a contract include: competent parties who

have legal capacity to make a contract; a proper subject matter that is not illegal or against public policy – for example, a contract to commit murder in exchange for money will not be enforced by the courts; consideration, which in most instances need not be pecuniary – most contracts are enforceable only if each party gets consideration from the agreement. Consideration can be money, property, a promise, or some right. For instance, when an owner sells studio equipment, the promised equipment is the consideration for the buyer. The seller's consideration is the money the buyer promises to pay for the equipment; mutuality of agreement or assent (meeting of the minds); mutual right to remedy – both parties must have an equal right to remedy upon breach of the terms by the other party; mutual obligation to perform – both parties must have some obligation to fulfill to the other (this can be distinct from consideration, which may be an initial inducement into the contract); and finally, absence of fraud or duress.

Long-term contracts are like rulebooks; they can be referred to periodically to refresh memories as to the conditions originally agreed upon. The contract may be express (either written or oral) or may be implied from circumstances. In general, contracts are either oral or written, however, oral contracts may be more difficult to enforce and to prove in a court of law. In order to be enforceable, certain classes of contracts must or should be written and signed. These include contracts involving the sale and transfer of real estate; contracts to guarantee or to answer for the miscarriage, debt, or default of another person; and, contracts for the sale of goods above a certain value. If the parties intend to draw up a written contract, they may shake hands on a general deal before all the specific terms have been defined. In some cases, legal obligations are created by the handshake or by other actions performed prior to the signing of a formal document. After the contract has been formed, the parties may continue to negotiate the details of how it should be carried out, especially if the contract is complicated. In many such cases, the parties prefer to work out disagreements on their own rather than ask a court to resolve them. In these cases, the contract may serve only as general guidelines governing the future relationship between the parties.

Typically, the remedy for breach of contract is an award of monetary damages intended to restore the injured party to the economic position expected from performance of the promise. If one party breaches or fails to perform obligations under a contract, the party injured by the breach typically may recover monetary damages as compensation for the breach. In addition, if the breach of contract is "material," the injured party may be excused from performing any of its remaining obligations under the contract. Occasionally, a court will order a party to perform the promise or obligations under the contract, or refrain from further breach, or to compensate for the value bestowed.

Before an entertainment deal is made or a contract is formed, the parties usually discuss or negotiate its terms. I always tell my students and clients – negotiating is like dating; get to know your partner before tying the knot. Negotiation periods can be tense and last quite a long period of time. Turn this negative into a positive. The negotiating process allows both parties to discover different sides to their future co-contractor or partner. This revealing procedure leads either to long-term productive agreements or to deals ending before they ever start. One should always remember that the best deals are sometimes the ones that don't get signed.

I shall now share my general entertainment negotiating principles. These basic tenants can help parties build successful deals and relationships in all the entertainment fields. The principles are simple and direct but often overlooked when doing business.

The first principle is the GREAT TRADE-OFF. When "artists" are born, they own 100% of their talent and product. The "great trade-off" allows artists to commercialize their talent and product with the help of others; however, trade-offs are risky, tricky, and have many pitfalls. Building a career in show business is like building a house; you can do all the construction work yourself or you can hire professionals to do the work. You can assume all the costs and own 100% of the house or share the costs and co-own the house with other investors. Fifty percent of something is better than one hundred percent of nothing. Keeping one hundred percent of all rights and property may lead to one hundred percent of nothing if the rights and property are not properly developed and commercially exploited. Trading one's rights and property (for example, copyrights) is an extremely painful experience, especially for authors and creators who have a personal attachment to the works they have created. However, in order to commercialize works and talent, help is often needed in the form of "time, effort and money". Unless professional help is paid for or adequately compensated, a trade-off may be necessary. This trade-off is a "great" gesture or compromise for anyone to make. When properly considered, an exchange of property and rights for quality "blood, sweat and tears" may be extremely beneficial and produce both short and long-term dividends. Trade-offs may also attract needed start-up money, investments or "seed capital". Never say never, always keep an open mind to the advantages of parting with cherished property.

The second principle is NEGOTIATING POWER. Use objectivity and identify which party has the most legitimate negotiating power. This will go a long way in helping parties determine the terms and conditions of a contract. For example, an unknown singer may have to give a well-known and successful personal manager a higher than average commission in order to secure his/her services.

The third principle is COMMON SENSE. A realistic view of the facts is crucial. Common sense helps parties accept the realities of a given situation and will provide them with the acumen to properly evaluate the need for a trade-off or judge the relative negotiating power of the parties. For instance, if an unknown and inexperienced actor demands millions of dollars from a small film studio for a secondary role, this lack of common sense may prevent the deal from getting done.

The fourth principle is FAIR AND BALANCED. Never abuse negotiating power. Although tempting, do not take advantage of another party's weakness, vulnerability, youth and inexperience, lack of representation, or unbridled enthusiasm. This does not mean that aggressive negotiating is discouraged, not at all; however never cross the "fairness" line into the "abusive" zone. This zone may deliver a great deal on paper, but short-term gain is not worth the long-term darkening to one's business reputation. For example, if a powerful book publisher offers a young, talented but naïve writer a contract, the enthusiastic and flattered writer may be ready to accept any conditions. The publisher should nevertheless offer the standard, industry acceptable minimums. The publisher should also encourage the writer to seek appropriate specialized legal representation in order to confirm the fairness of its offer. If not, this writer will surely one day realize the abusive nature of the relationship and may speak negatively about the publisher to the press, colleagues, and peers. The writer may also refuse to consider working with the publisher on future projects. A fair and balanced approach to negotiations will generally pay-off in the long-term.

The fifth and final principle is BETTER SAFE THAN SORRY. Always get a qualified professional to negotiate or at least review a contract before signing it. Although costs may be involved, an experienced manager, agent, or entertainment lawyer should be consulted. Entertainment lawyers negotiate, draft, and help enforce contracts. Lawyers are like dentists. Yes, they may be painful and costly, however, preventive measures will usually save time and money in the long run. Regular dentist check-ups and maintenance are relatively inexpensive compared to painful and expensive, major tooth repair down the road. Hiring someone to review an unsigned bad contract will cost little compared to living with a signed bad contract. Clauses, sentences, words, and even commas have important implications in contracts. One word in a forty-page agreement can translate into thousands of dollars. For example, the difference between the words "gross" and "net" are substantial. Commissions based on gross revenues (before expenses) are much greater than commissions based on net revenues (after expenses). Entertainment careers, enterprises, and projects are worth protecting in the same way as people protect their houses. Both demand an investment in time and money. It is foolish for a home owner to personally replace the plumbing system without at least having a licensed plumber review the work before covering up the walls and ceiling. A water leak caused by the homeowner's mistake will end up costing much more than the plumber's initial fee. In other words – pay now or risk paying much more, later.

In addition to the above-mentioned general principles, the following industry "truths" should also be considered when building an entertainment career or business.

One should NEVER BE IN A RUSH TO FAIL. Although it is quite tempting to enter into what seems to be an excellent opportunity or deal, take the appropriate time to consider and review all the implications. For example, musicians should not quickly send off a poorly recorded demo of their songs to potential record companies or managers. Always present one's best and most refined product or ideas to others, this might be the only opportunity one gets. Sometimes a failed first impression will be the last.

TRUST BUT VERIFY. Trust is important in the entertainment business-world, however, always confirm one's trust and verify its validity. In doing so, parties will either avert bad deals or solidify fledgling relationships. As a general rule: doubt what you hear, trust what you see.

MAKING MONEY AND GETTING PAID ARE TWO DIFFERENT THINGS. Although working in the entertainment field is exciting and fulfilling, monetary compensation is a key factor. All entertainment industries have a "revenue food chain" or a trickling down of the customer's money into the hands of those who are selling and creating products. Always position yourself securely in the food chain in order to guarantee payment. Contracts or arrangements describe how parties make money via royalties, commissions, fees, and other forms of remuneration; receiving currency or payment, however, isn't always so clear. For example, the revenue food chain may place a music-recording artist at the bottom. Customers will buy the artist's record from a retail store, which purchased the record from a wholesaler, which bought it from a distributor, which pays the record company, which finally compensates the artist. If the chain gets broken at one point (due to bankruptcy or dishonesty), the artist will not get paid. Prepayment of royalties, salaries, advances or other forms of advanced or guaranteed payments will help prevent this most important of entertainment industry truths.

## ESSENTIALS OF ENTERTAINMENT CONTRACTS

**CAPACITY**
**SUBJECT MATTER**
**CONSIDERATION**
**MUTUAL AGREEMENT**
**ABSENCE OF FRAUD OR DURESS**
**MUTUAL RIGHT TO REMEDY**

## GENERAL ENTERTAINMENT NEGOTIATING PRINCIPLES

**GREAT TRADE-OFF**
**NEGOTIATING POWER**
**COMMON SENSE**
**FAIR AND BALANCED**
**BETTER SAFE THAN SORRY**

title – date – location – names of parties – preamble – nature/ grant of rights & services – scope/purpose/mandate – term/ period/duration – options – renewal – territory – definitions – appointment/delegation – confidentiality – non-competition – obligations/duties/responsibilities/performance – exclusivity – contributions – license – non-performance – penalties – fee/salary/ remuneration/royalties/commission – expenses/revenues (net vs. gross) – signing & performance bonus/advance – loans – payment schedule – foreign sales/income/currency – accounting – audit/ inspection – distribution – merchandising – licenses – endorsements – sponsorships – copyright – trademarks – international markets – customs broker – quality control – finished product – broadcast rights – approval/veto/consultation – division of profits/loses – books & records – morality/criminality/public policy – product sell-off/ recall – warehousing – destruction of product – consumer packaging/ labeling/safety – product liability – insurance – photographs/ illustrations/artwork/graphic designs – name/trademark ownership – recoupment – sunset – leaving/new group member – dissolution – withdrawal – limited liability –performance/reproduction/ mecanical/synchronization/print/subsidiary/private copy rights – cross collateralization – artist life insurance – breach & waiver – bankruptcy – power of attorney – cancellation – ancillary rights – merchandising rights – rider – import/export – off-stage sales – e-commerce – credits – consignment – amendments – arbitration/ mediation – assignment – bankruptcy – default/cure/remedy – revocability – termination – extension – survival of rights/duties/ obligations – option to purchase/sell – transfer of rights/property – trust management – key person – regulations – warranty/guarantee/ representations – indemnification/compensation – disclosure – restrictive covenants entity – force majeur – governing law – entire agreement – enurement/heirs/successors/assigns – injunctive relief – minors – no agency – notices – construction – severability – no partnership – notwithstanding – unions & guilds – miscellaneous – applicable/governing laws – jurisdiction – independent legal advice – choice of language – witnesses – signing/applicable/effective dates

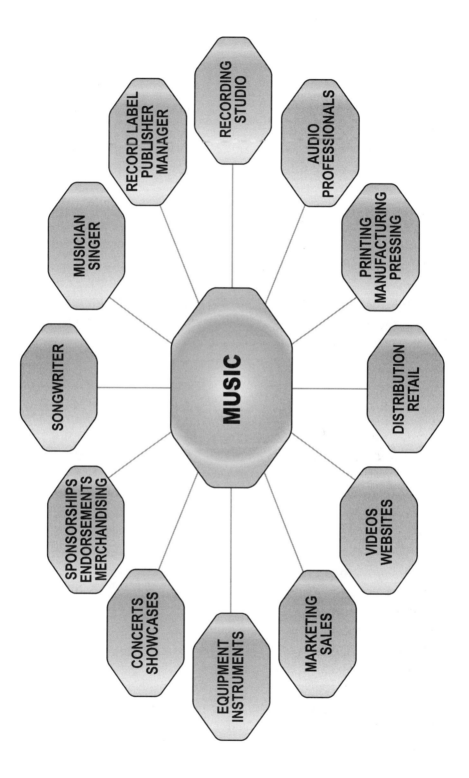

MUSIC

RECORDING STUDIO

RECORD LABEL PUBLISHER MANAGER

AUDIO PROFESSIONALS

MUSICIAN SINGER

PRINTING MANUFACTURING PRESSING

SONGWRITER

DISTRIBUTION RETAIL

SPONSORSHIPS ENDORSEMENTS MERCHANDISING

VIDEOS WEBSITES

CONCERTS SHOWCASES

EQUIPMENT INSTRUMENTS

MARKETING SALES

# 4.   MUSIC

The Music Industry is a branch of commercial trade dealing with the production and sale of musical recordings, music publishing, live musical performances, and related merchandise. Furthermore, the music business interconnects and interrelates with the different industries encompassed by the business of international entertainment.

The center of the music business universe is the artist (singer and/or musician), around which all activities revolve. Its core is the song. Artists interpret or play music composed by themselves or others. Simply put, all music industry revenue, jobs, and careers emanate from the artist. When the artist is a group, partnership agreements tend to be the most popular form of legal arrangement, particularly in the early stages of a band's career. Furthermore, many of the same considerations arise in the context of incorporating, and generally, a band can incorporate from a partnership, when and if the need arises.

Making a musical recording involves many people besides the musicians and singers, whose music appears on the recording. A&R (artist and repertoire), sound engineers, producers, managers, and salespeople all combine to bring musical recordings to consumers. A&R personnel represent the record label. They focus on talent scouting and artist/career/product development. Personal managers are like quarterbacks or head coaches; they oversee all the different aspects and activities of an artist's career. Recording personnel or audio professionals include engineers who coordinate the technical aspects of recording. Recording engineers operate the recording equipment and ensure that the acoustics of the recording are of the highest quality possible. Mix engineers specialize in combining, or mixing, tracks that have already been recorded. These engineers balance the musical parts and make final alterations to the sound qualities of the voices or musical instruments. Mastering engineers supervise the final recording of a musical selection into a seamless and unified, artistic whole. They make final adjustments to sound quality and work out transitions between pieces of music.

Record producers are responsible for the artistic aspects of a recording. They are concerned about the musical quality of the performance and make certain that the artists are performing at their highest level. The record producer is also generally responsible for project management, overseeing the recording budget, and coordinating the personnel involved in making the recordings.

Record labels are the enterprises that bring the recording to the public. They are responsible for manufacturing the recording and printing the packaging. Labels market and advertise the recording and ship it through distributors to retail stores, or in the case of digital files they make the recording available to online retailers. Record labels also invest time, effort, and money in discovering new talent and developing the talent of musicians already under contract with them. Labels and distributors generally fall into two main categories: major and independent. Major record labels are multinational corporations with extensive resources and worldwide distribution networks. As a result of corporate mergers, few major labels remain. Independent record labels and distributors constitute thousands of enterprises, big and small, that are not owned by the major labels. Independent labels, however, often make arrangements with major distributors for the distribution of their products.

A recording is made in a recording studio. Studios range from transformed storage rooms, basements or garages to multimillion-dollar facilities with state-of-the-art equipment. Professional recording studios contain two types of rooms: performance spaces and control rooms. Performance spaces should be acoustically isolated so that external sounds are not recorded. Many studios also have small booths where individual performers can be separated from one another. Some home studios have no formal performance areas but have one space that serves both as a control room and as a performance space. Musical instrument digital interface (MIDI) studios have no need for performance spaces, as all sounds are electronically generated.

The control room contains the recording equipment and mixing console and is usually adjacent to the performance space. A window between the two spaces allows eye contact between the performers and the engineer. The mixing console is the central component where all of the recording devices are interconnected. Depending on the complexity of the recording, these devices might include microphones, multitrack recorders, computers, synchronization devices, and units that electronically alter sounds called signal processors.

A recording starts with the sound source, usually someone singing or playing an instrument. The performers' sounds are captured by microphones and directed into a physical/virtual mixing console or computer soundcards. Electronically produced sounds, such as those from synthesizers or electric guitars, are sent directly into the mixing console. The mixing console serves as the central element of the recording studio. The console directs signals from one location to another, allows engineers to control the balance and sound qualities of signals, and allows engineers to monitor the signals in many different ways. When a sound reaches the mixing console immediately after a performance, it is most often routed to a multi-track recorder. There, the sound from each instrument or voice is placed on its own track, where each individual sound can be accessed again later. Once all of the performances have been assembled on the tracks of the recorder, a mix engineer takes the reins.

The sounds from the multi-track recorder are then played back through the mixing console. The mix engineer works with the producer to select the materials that will appear in the final cohesive version of the recording. The engineer shapes the final sound qualities of the voices and instruments by signal processing and establishes the loudness levels of the instruments in relationship to one another. When this process is completed, the recording exists in its final form.

Often, recordings are made specifically for radio, television, or motion picture use. In these cases a record label may not be involved. Production companies or individual entrepreneurs copyright the recordings and distribute them directly to the radio, television, or motion picture producers. Such recordings are usually made in recording studios, but the means by which these recordings are brought to market differ for each project.

In order to satisfy the public's growing demand for music, the music industry must constantly adapt to new forms of technology to ensure wide distribution, legal accessibility, and fair compensation. For example, dual disks offer music lovers a more multi-dimensional, personal connection to their favorite artist, allowing fans to buy a CD that has a DVD included on the other side of the disk. Also, major labels are making significant commitments towards capitalizing on the worldwide technological demand for music and entertainment content on mobile portable devices. For example, content and operating services are offered to telcos and service providers. These include the entire range of mobile personalization services: master tones, ringbacks/ringtones, multimedia messaging service, voicemail greetings, and games.

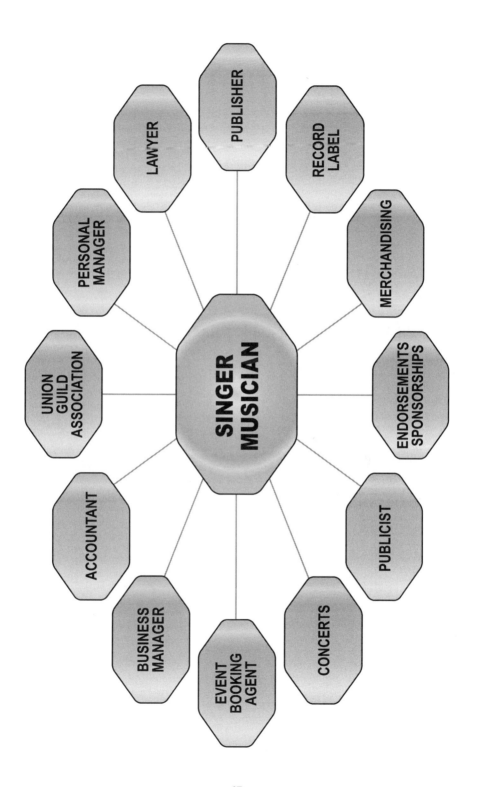

SINGER MUSICIAN

- PUBLISHER
- LAWYER
- RECORD LABEL
- PERSONAL MANAGER
- MERCHANDISING
- UNION GUILD ASSOCIATION
- ENDORSEMENTS SPONSORSHIPS
- ACCOUNTANT
- PUBLICIST
- BUSINESS MANAGER
- EVENT BOOKING AGENT
- CONCERTS

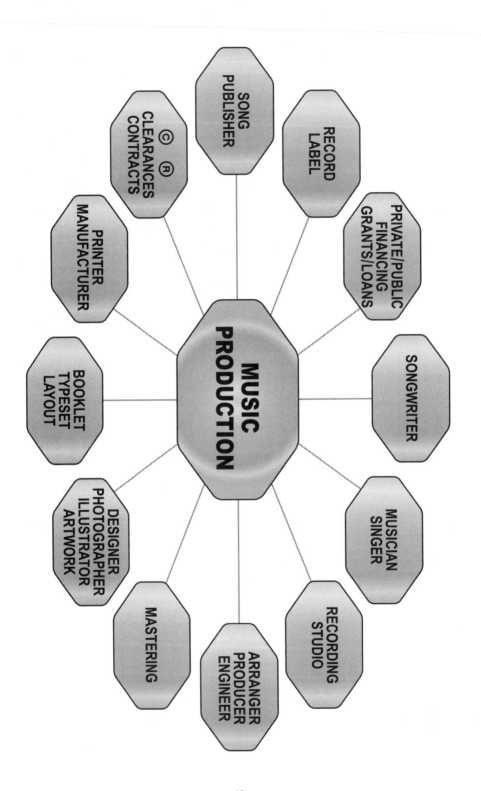

MUSIC PRODUCTION

- SONG PUBLISHER
- RECORD LABEL
- PRIVATE/PUBLIC FINANCING GRANTS/LOANS
- SONGWRITER
- MUSICIAN SINGER
- RECORDING STUDIO
- ARRANGER PRODUCER ENGINEER
- MASTERING
- DESIGNER PHOTOGRAPHER ILLUSTRATOR ARTWORK
- BOOKLET TYPESET LAYOUT
- PRINTER MANUFACTURER
- CLEARANCES CONTRACTS © ®

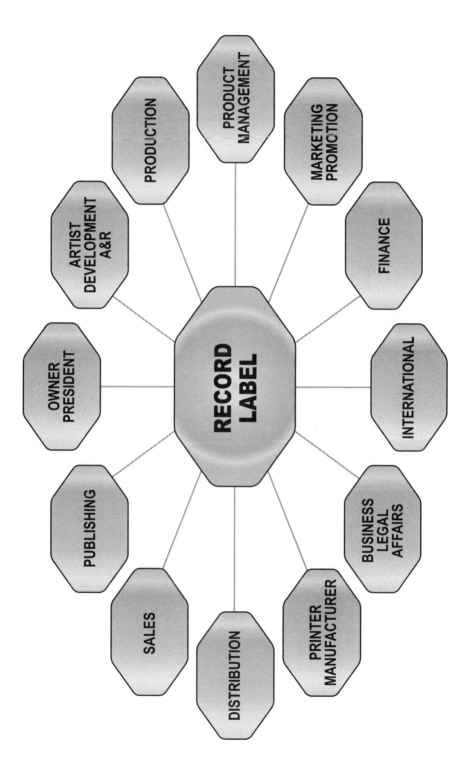

RECORD LABEL

- PRODUCT MANAGEMENT
- PRODUCTION
- MARKETING PROMOTION
- ARTIST DEVELOPMENT A&R
- FINANCE
- OWNER PRESIDENT
- INTERNATIONAL
- PUBLISHING
- BUSINESS LEGAL AFFAIRS
- SALES
- PRINTER MANUFACTURER
- DISTRIBUTION

Music publishing is the exploitation, promotion, protection, and administration of musical copyrights that the publisher owns and controls by virtue of the assignment of rights granted pursuant to a publishing contract. Simply put, music publishers are song managers. Songs are assets that generate revenues; there may be several who share the assets and/or revenues but usually only one who administrates and controls the destiny of the songs. Everyone wants a piece of music publishing. Although songwriters may give-up the ownership and control of their songs, they generally continue to receive a minimum of 50% of all revenues.

## MUSIC PUBLISHER'S TASKS

CREATIVE / PROMOTIONAL / BUSINESS / ADMINISTRATIVE

The creative tasks include assisting in the development of a composer's writing talent, recording demos, suggesting appropriate modifications, adaptations, or translations of songs, and arranging collaborations with lyricists, composers, and arrangers. The promotional tasks consist of approaching entertainment industry people who may be interested in a license to use the musical copyrights owned or controlled by the publisher. Business tasks include investing in talent and demos, negotiating and drafting agreements, and the supervision of copyright protection. The administrative tasks include copyright registration, collection and payment of royalties, and general accounting.

## TYPES OF MUSIC PUBLISHING CONTACTS

**SONGWRITER & PUBLISHER SINGLE-SONG
SONGWRITER & PUBLISHER EXCLUSIVE TERM
SINGLE-SONG or CATALOGUE ADMINISTRATION
CO-PUBLISHING / SUB-PUBLISHING / JOINT PUBLISHING
SALE OF SINGLE-SONG or CATALOGUE**

## TYPES OF MUSIC PUBLISHING LICENSES

**PERFORMANCE / REPRODUCTION (Mechanical)
SYNCHRONIZATION / PRINT / SUBSIDIARY**

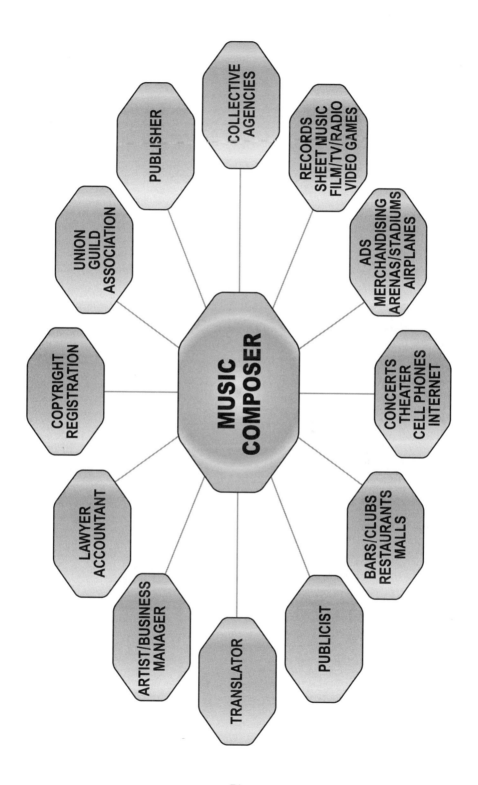

71

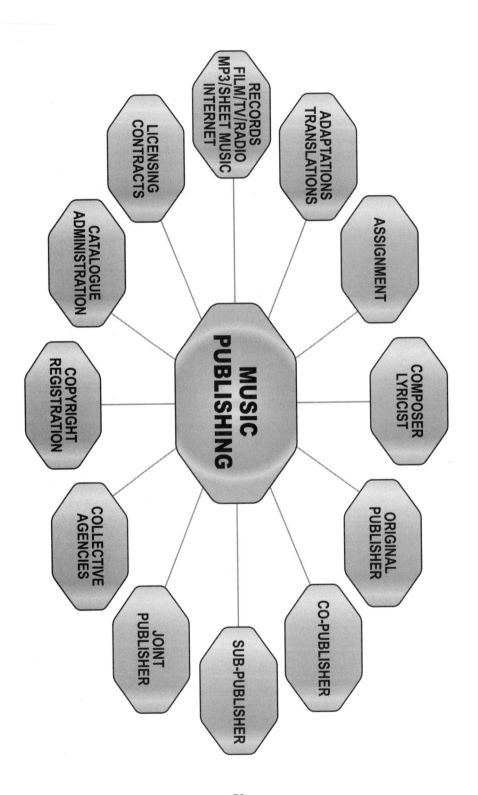

MUSIC PUBLISHING

- RECORDS FILM/TV/RADIO MP3/SHEET MUSIC INTERNET
- ADAPTATIONS TRANSLATIONS
- ASSIGNMENT
- COMPOSER LYRICIST
- ORIGINAL PUBLISHER
- CO-PUBLISHER
- SUB-PUBLISHER
- JOINT PUBLISHER
- COLLECTIVE AGENCIES
- COPYRIGHT REGISTRATION
- CATALOGUE ADMINISTRATION
- LICENSING CONTRACTS

# KEY MUSIC INDUSTRY CONTRACTS

ORGANIZATION OF RECORDING ARTISTS – GROUP MEMBERS ENTERPRISE/PARTNERSHIP/SHAREHOLDER – EMPLOYMENT OF BAND MEMBERS – RECORDING ARTISTS' NAMES – EXCLUSIVE TERM RECORDING – ARTIST DEVELOPMENT – COMPILATION ALBUM – RECORD PRODUCER & RECORD COMPANY – ALBUM CONCEPT/COVER ART/DESIGN/PHOTOGRAPHS – ALBUM MANUFACTURING – DISTRIBUTION – P&D (PRESSING AND DISTRIBUTION) – FINDER'S FEE – INTERNET MUSIC SALES – LICENSING RECORD MASTERS – MASTERS PURCHASE/SALE – MUSIC VIDEO PRODUCTION – MASTER REMIX – RETAIL MERCHANDISING – ARTIST/TOUR/ EVENT SPONSORSHIP – PRODUCT ENDORSEMENT – STUDIO ENGINEER SERVICES – PUBLISHING/COPYRIGHT – TRADEMARK LICENSE – PERSONAL/BUSINESS MANAGEMENT – PERSONAL AGENT – LIVE PERFORMANCE – CONCERT BOOKING AGENT – SINGLE ENGAGEMENT – EXTENDED ENGAGEMENT – TOURS – CONCERT AND TOUR RELATED SERVICES AND EQUIPMENT – TOUR MERCHANDISE LICENSING – PERSONAL APPEARANCES – EXCHANGE OF SERVICES – FILM MUSIC AGREEMENT – MOVIE SOUNDTRACK – ADVERTISING/JINGLE MUSIC – WORK-FOR-HIRE – STUDIO/LIVE MUSICIAN – VIDEO GAME SOUNDTRACK – TELEVISION SOUNDTRACK – TELEVISION SERIES COMPOSER – MUSICIAN UNION/ GUILD – WAIVER/RELEASE/PERMISSION – E-COMMERCE DESIGN/DEVELOPMENT/SERVICING – MUSIC SOFTWARE – MUSIC FRANCHISE – CONSIGNMENT – MUSIC FESTIVAL PERFORMANCE – SAMPLING – SONG ARRANGEMENT – AUDIO PROFESSIONALS – STUDIO MUSICIAN – LIVE MUSICAL THEATER – MUSICAL THEATER CAST ALBUM – ARTIST RIGHTS COLLECTION AGENCY AFFILIATION – KARAOKE – WEBSITE CONSTRUCTION/MAINTENANCE – REVERSION OF RIGHTS – TERMINATION/FINAL RELEASE

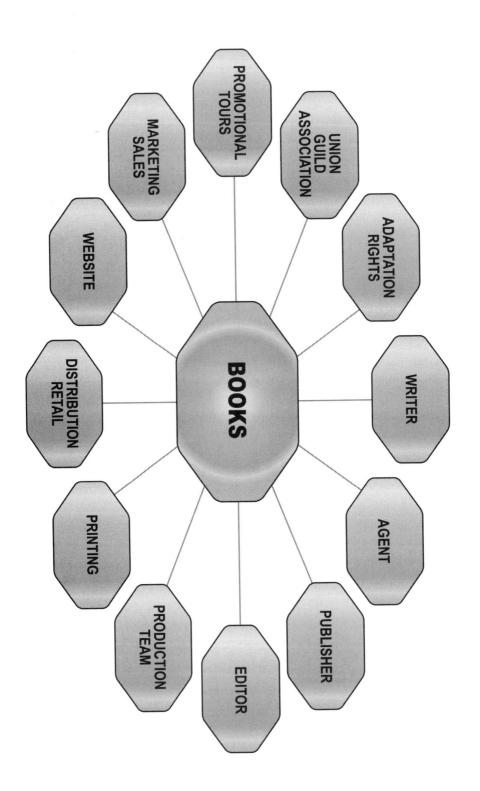

BOOKS

- PROMOTIONAL TOURS
- MARKETING SALES
- UNION GUILD ASSOCIATION
- WEBSITE
- ADAPTATION RIGHTS
- DISTRIBUTION RETAIL
- WRITER
- PRINTING
- AGENT
- PRODUCTION TEAM
- EDITOR
- PUBLISHER

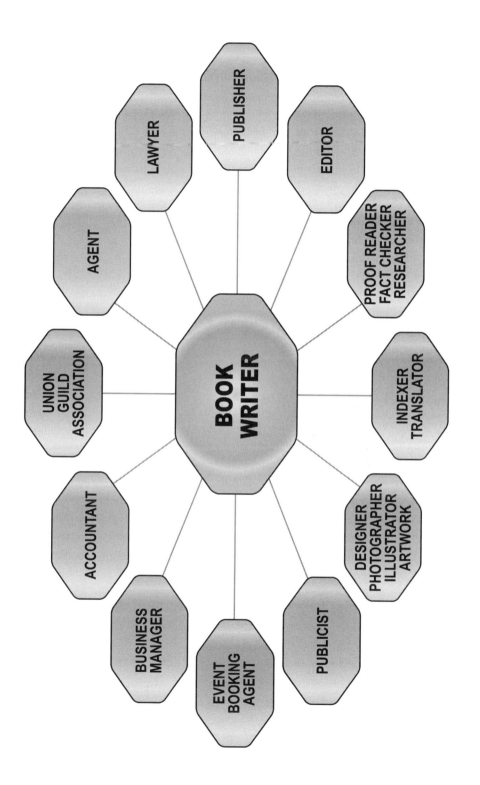

BOOK WRITER

PUBLISHER

LAWYER

EDITOR

AGENT

PROOF READER
FACT CHECKER
RESEARCHER

UNION
GUILD
ASSOCIATION

INDEXER
TRANSLATOR

ACCOUNTANT

DESIGNER
PHOTOGRAPHER
ILLUSTRATOR
ARTWORK

BUSINESS
MANAGER

EVENT
BOOKING
AGENT

PUBLICIST

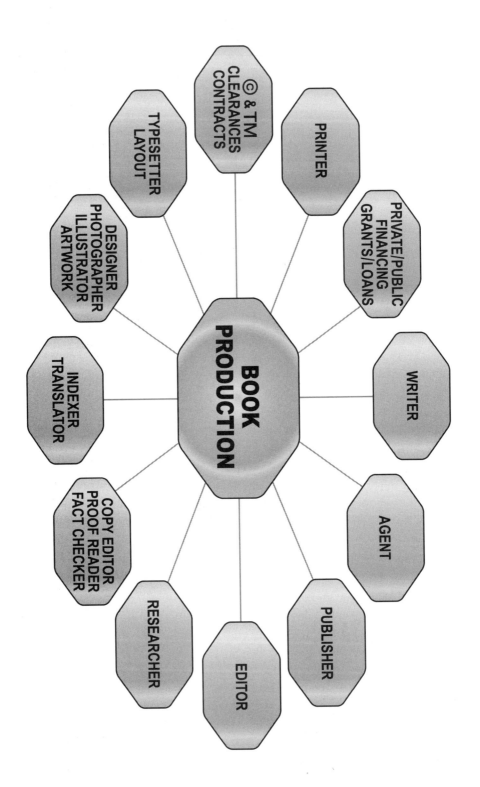

BOOK PRODUCTION

© & TM CLEARANCES CONTRACTS

PRINTER

PRIVATE/PUBLIC FINANCING GRANTS/LOANS

WRITER

AGENT

PUBLISHER

EDITOR

RESEARCHER

COPY EDITOR PROOF READER FACT CHECKER

INDEXER TRANSLATOR

DESIGNER PHOTOGRAPHER ILLUSTRATOR ARTWORK

TYPESETTER LAYOUT

# 5. BOOKS

Prior to Gutenberg and the age of the book, the world lived in a pictorial age. Since then, the printed word has enlightened, informed, educated, and entertained the masses. Still today, the printed book and book industry constitute the foundation of the entertainment industry.

In simple terms, "to publish" means to "make public," "to circulate or to make known to the public in general." Book publishing is the manufacture, publication, marketing, and distribution of books. Approximately twenty-five percent of book publishing is the general fiction and nonfiction trade books that are advertised and reviewed in the mass media, displayed/sold in bookstores and online, and charted on the best-seller lists. The other seventy-five percent includes business, educational, technical, scientific and reference book publishing.

Trade books carry on the literary tradition, and often create the public image, of a publishing house. They may support a house's other publishing activities or ventures and are usually less expensive to produce per unit than textbooks. The non-trade hard cover textbook and reference book department, however, is often the profit-making division of the publishing house. Textbook publishing alone constitutes a large part of the industry. In North American publishing, one-quarter of all revenues are from textbooks. Many publishers are devoted entirely to one of many specialized textbook publishing fields, such as religious and medical reference books. Additionally, some professional, technical, and scientific works are sold as textbooks. University presses focus on scholarly works and are thus quite active in this market.

Mass-market publishing dominates the book industry. Such publishing may be defined as the development, distributing, marketing, and selling of hard and soft cover books that are intended for larger audiences. Mass-market titles are sold through the traditional retail channels of bookstores, as well as online, in newsstands, supermarkets, stationery and department stores, drugstores, and airports. The enormous success of mass-market publishing is reflected in the large advances against royalties offered for reprint rights of best-selling novels by the highly competitive paperback houses. A division of a general publisher may issue paperback lines or houses specializing in paperbacks may produce them.

No matter what kind of book is being produced, the editorial and production process is substantially the same. In the case of general trade books, a publishing house will plan to issue a list of titles ranging in number from 4 to 6 in the smallest firms to as many as 500 or more in the largest. A few books are bought from the thousands of unsolicited manuscripts that the major houses receive yearly, but most come from either outlines or manuscripts submitted by recognized literary agents or entertainment lawyers. A large number of books also originate within the house, as editors develop ideas and find writers to author the books. Writers receive royalties at rates varying with the amount of books sold; the more books sold, the greater the percentage of profit for both author and publisher. The typical trade book generally breaks even (by covering the cost of its production, marketing, and distribution) when five to ten thousand copies have been sold.

Once the publisher receives a requested manuscript, the editor takes over. Editors usually work with several books at once, and in many publishing houses they are responsible for every phase of book production. Editors may work with writers by suggesting changes in a manuscript, or they may do line-by-line editing, reviewing the changes with the writers later.

Finished manuscripts must be copy edited before they can go into production. Copy editors prepare the book for the digital computer typesetter, correcting spelling/grammar and also questioning the writers on possible errors of meaning or fact, and internal structural difficulties. Copy editors do meticulous research as they work, consulting reference sources to be certain the writer's facts are correct. In-house lawyers often vet potentially controversial subject matter prior to publication. Once on the market, books are liable to confront legal problems. Textbooks are often challenged on political, religious, moral, and sexual grounds. Books are also challenged in court on grounds of plagiarism, invasion of privacy, and defamation of character or liable.

Design is the next step in production, usually done within the publishing house or by freelance designers. The designer plans the book's format including: type/quality of paper; page size; number of lines on a page; space between lines, words, and letters; borders; size/font style of type; color and arrangement of pictures; front/back cover, and spine.

The first step in the manufacturing stage is to set the book in type. Computer typesetting followed by complete automation of the printing and binding process allows publishers to quickly respond to market demands by easily printing small and large quantities, while remaining cost effective. These same technological advances have also led to the rise in self-publishing and books-on-demand.

Once the book is complete, it is ready for marketing and distribution. Targeted print and electronic media is key. Press releases and publisher's catalogue copy set the tone for any marketing campaign. Trade books are sold primarily by salespersons taking direct orders for forthcoming books from independent bookstores and chains. The two important selling seasons are fall and spring. Large publishers have their own sales staff, which is briefed by editors at sales conferences before working the phones/e-mails or going on the road. Independent commission salespeople, who may handle the titles of several houses, represent smaller publishers. Books are usually moved from publisher to bookseller through wholesale distributors. Retail book distributors of all types deal directly with individual bookstores, book departments in large department stores, major chain operations, and online booksellers. Increasingly, the chains, book clubs and major online retailers have come to dominate trade selling and are able to obtain big discounts from the publishers.

An adjunct of the publishing industry is the packager who devises individual titles and series of books to be produced and distributed by regular trade, text, or reference houses. International co-ventures are common for book projects that have extremely high development costs. Book clubs of all sizes are also a prime distribution source for books.

Competition for the global entertainment dollar is fierce, driving publishers and retailers to adopt aggressive marketing methods and techniques. The book trade has recently witnessed the growing incidence of mergers, particularly the acquisition of publishing houses by conglomerates. Families had traditionally run the book trade, with control passing from one generation to the next. Today, the largest book publishers are often simply divisions of even larger entertainment and communication conglomerates. Mass-market titles are marketed via a conglomerate's other entertainment entities such as television, films, Internet, video games, and music. Convergence and consolidation has greatly influenced and affected the nature of the book business.

The average publishing house deals with an overwhelming number of book submissions. Many books are found and bought out of what publishers call the "slush pile" of manuscripts. The major publishing houses deal almost exclusively with agents or specialized lawyers, and many will not even look at a proposal that is not submitted by an agent or attorney. One of an editor's main jobs is to keep in close contact with a group of agents and attorneys, letting them know what kind of books that editor is looking for, and getting them used to that editor's taste, priorities, and preferences. Ideally, a good agent or attorney will help put the final polish on a proposal, and will get it directly to the appropriate editors and publishers most likely to buy that kind of book and most likely to publish such a book successfully. Unfortunately, representatives, such as agents and attorneys, also must deal with a huge amount of proposals. Representatives need to move a lot of product, and they are often unable to give the kind of attention that writers might expect on a project. Some representatives stick with a project they believe in until the proper home is found, but many may run out of energy before reaching the ideal publisher.

For most new writers, an agent might not be practical or possible at first. Market instability or other factors might make agents reluctant to take on any new writers, no matter how well the author writes. Except for those publishing houses that deal exclusively with agents, lawyers, or by invitation, authors don't really need an agent to submit work for publication consideration. Authors can do most everything an agent does, though an agent will have better knowledge of the market and what the publishing houses are buying. A few well-known authors sold their first books without agents.

As previously mentioned, however, most major publishers will not look at a book unless it comes from a literary agent or entertainment lawyer. That means an author needs to find an agent willing to represent his/her work. Most authors are thrilled when any agent offers to represent them. Having the wrong agent, however, can be worse than having no agent at all. Thousands of people in North America call themselves agents. About 10% of those make 90% of the deals. The biggest deals tend to go to the same few agents. Without this knowledge, an author can end up signing on with someone who doesn't know how to get the most money a manuscript can command. Agents with poor track records often charge reading fees, or have few or no contacts in the publishing world, or refer clients to vanity or subsidy publishers that require authors to underwrite either a partial or total amount of publishing and promoting their book. In these cases, the risk to the publisher is nominal, enabling them to accept many manuscripts that conventional publishers reject as a poor investment.

Many writers believe they need a literary agent or entertainment lawyer to sell their book manuscript. Although this is usually the case with the major publishers, many smaller companies often deal directly with the author. For those who want an agent, it makes sense to know something about how it works. First off, reputable agents don't charge a reader fee or fee up front to represent clients. They earn their living by selling books to a publisher and gaining a commission. That commission is a percentage of the proceeds a book earns. For one thing, this gives the agent an incentive to actually shop the book around to various publishers likely to buy it for publication. This is another reason why many agents scrutinize submissions carefully. They know what publishers are looking for. Therefore, like the publishers, they're unlikely to accept anything that isn't ready or almost ready for submission. Most agents do not represent short stories unless they're in an anthology for publishing as a book. There simply isn't enough money paid for short stories so that an agent can earn a living. Authors of short stories should plan on sending their work directly to publishers.

Like any marketplace, agents have differing commission rates. There are some costs that a reputable agent might pass on to the author before a manuscript is sold. Such costs as copying the manuscript, postage, and long distance calls to publishers on the author's behalf are often typical. Authors should ensure that the agent documents each expense and keeps the costs within reason. Any charge made to the author that is payable prior to the sale of the manuscript to a publisher, is a "fee" and represents inappropriate conduct not in the author's best interest. If a manuscript is truly marketable in the agent's opinion but needs editing, most good agents will recommend a few editing services for authors to meet and choose from. As well, a good agent might even steer clients away from any editing service known to be a scam. Some agents have even been known to go above and beyond the call of duty in assisting with the editing themselves when they feel they have a sure winner to represent. However, authors should ensure that their manuscript is edited prior to submitting it to any agent or publisher.

In addition to being the one responsible for getting the best deal with any publishing house, the agent is also an author's money manager. When a manuscript sells to a publisher, the agent is the one who receives the money. The agent then subtracts the appropriate commission and pays the author the remainder.

Many smaller and more specialized houses pay attention to unsolicited manuscripts. The paperback romance publishers, for example, regularly enlist new authors from the ranks of their submissions pile. Many publishers in the industry are independent small and mid-sized businesses spread throughout North America. These companies are often much more accustomed and open to doing business with unpublished writers. They are often the houses that thrive on finding and developing new talent. Many writers find, however, that even if they can secure an interested publisher without an agent, that it is still recommended that they retain an agent or attorney to close the deal. First-time authors often are reluctant to pay a percentage of their earnings to an agent. If a deal is relatively simple, or the potential of the book high, the author may prefer to pay an entertainment lawyer by the hour rather than pay an agent by the percentage.

Reference books, websites, industry associations, unions, guilds, libraries, and bookstores will help writers find up-to-date lists of publishers, editors, agents, and specialized lawyers. Some of these book industry people and companies list their specialties, and their appropriate manuscript submission requirements. The best way to find the right collaborator is by comparing one's manuscript to other similar published works. For example, chances are good that the editor and agent of someone else's sports book might be interested in yours as well. The closer a comparison one can make in subject, or sensibility, or style of presentation, the better the chances that an author will connect with the right people. Authors should look at the copyright or acknowledgments pages of a book to see if the editor or agent is credited. Bookstores are a great place for research. Authors should look closely at the category in which their book would be sold. Writers should try to notice which publishers dominate the category with their books facing out on the store-shelf, and stocked in large quantities. Individual titles also reveal how successful publishers have been. For example, check the inside title or copyright page, and look for a small sequence of numbers at the bottom of the page. This indicates what printing the copy of the book comes from – the more printings, the more successful the title. Finally, one should talk to local booksellers and librarians. They are generally very supportive of authors, and often enjoy sharing their opinions on which publishers are the best in different fields.

Publishers, editors, and agents enjoy dealing with educated writers who know their market. When approaching publishing houses for contact information, the editorial department should know the editor's name, and the sub-rights or publicity departments should know the individual who "agented" the book. When writing to these people, authors should make it very clear why they were identified as likely candidates for their manuscript or idea submission. Always obtain an editor's name before submitting a proposal. Sending a proposal to the Editorial Department or to an editor who does not know the author is often futile. When sending a proposal, let the recipient know why they were targeted by referring to other books published by that recipient that are similar in some fashion to the submission. When contacting publishers who deal by invitation only, an inquiry letter should be used. If an inquiry letter gains the publisher's interest, the publisher will then request to see a manuscript.

When putting together a book proposal, authors should be organized, clear, and to the point. This is a sales presentation, therefore, how a proposal looks, and how professionally it is presented, is critical to shaping the attitude with which the proposal will be viewed. As a general rule, one should include a one-page cover letter and an introduction that presents the idea in two pages or less explaining what the book is about, what makes it unique, what the market is, and how it will be reached. A table of contents should be included, annotated if necessary, to give an overall picture of the book. Sample material, enough to convince, and enough to give a sense of what they are buying. A photograph and information about the author explaining what makes him/her the right author to do this book. And finally, a marketing plan should be included. How can the author help sell this book, what special places and ways can it be sold, and what special ways can it be promoted.

Although book proposal ideas are rarely stolen, copyright protection should be ensured, prior to any submissions. As previously explained in this tome, copyright protection does not apply to a book idea or a title. Copyright protection applies to an entire work. Occasionally, series titles will enjoy some trademark protection. When a publisher evaluates a proposal, they look at the idea to see if they like it, and they look at the author and sample materials to see if they think the execution can live up to the promise of the idea.

Once a publishing house is interested in an author's book idea or completed work, a publishing contract will be offered. Though terms vary, the general parameters of a typical book deal tend to fall within a standard range. Both traditional agents and attorneys acting as agents negotiate contracts for paperback or serialization rights, as well as for television, film, dramatic, and subsidiary rights

Most publishers will offer some form of non-refundable advance, applied against royalties accrued on all sales. Advances constitute a portion of what publishers conservatively think the author will earn within the first years of publication. Advances have little to do with the time and effort invested in writing the book. Advances constitute a risk for publishers. According to the potential sales for the book, advances can range from a few thousand dollars to millions of dollars. Most book advances are between $5000 and $10,000. Fewer than 10% of all book advances are six figures or more. Royalties are generally a percentage of the retail price on trade paperbacks, mass-market paperbacks, and hard covers. Coffee-table books and reference books often require more investment and production work upfront, and yield lower advances. When publishers invest more editorial and artistic effort, lower royalties are offered.

Book Publishing is a highly competitive and skilled industry in which editorial judgment must be coupled with business, marketing, and administrative acumen, judgment, and skills in order to make large and small investments bear fruit. From an industry composed essentially of small, family-held firms, book publishing in North America has grown into a complex component of the field of international entertainment and communications.

*In simple terms, "to publish" means to "make public,"*
*"to circulate or to make known to the public in general."*

*Book publishing is the manufacture,*
*publication, marketing, and distribution of books.*

## BOOK PROPOSAL

### COVER LETTER
### INTRODUCTION
### TABLE OF CONTENTS
### SAMPLE MATERIAL
### AUTHOR BIO & PHOTO
### MARKETING PLAN

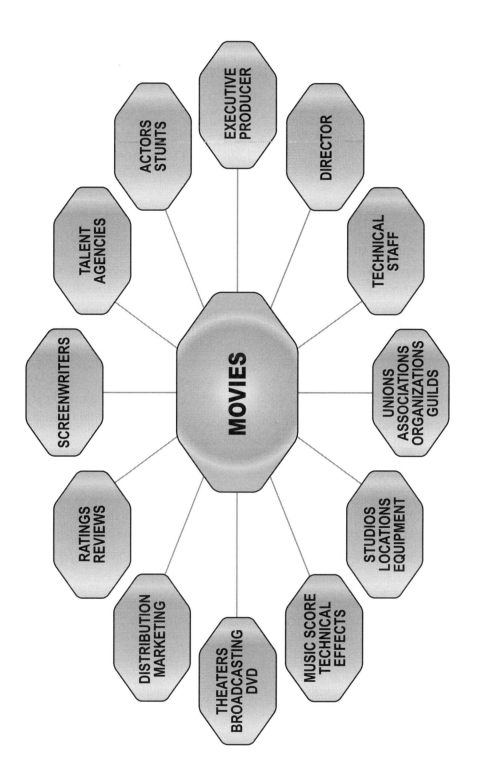

MOVIES

- EXECUTIVE PRODUCER
- ACTORS STUNTS
- TALENT AGENCIES
- SCREENWRITERS
- RATINGS REVIEWS
- DISTRIBUTION MARKETING
- THEATERS BROADCASTING DVD
- MUSIC SCORE TECHNICAL EFFECTS
- STUDIOS LOCATIONS EQUIPMENT
- UNIONS ASSOCIATIONS ORGANIZATIONS GUILDS
- TECHNICAL STAFF
- DIRECTOR

# 6.   MOVIES

Movies – also called motion pictures, pictures, films, or cinema – are one of the most popular types of entertainment. In all its forms, cinema is an art as well as a business. There are many kinds of motion pictures, but the most significant categories are feature films, animated films, industrial films, experimental films, documentaries, and educational films.

The film industry comprises all of the studios, laboratories, agencies, firms, and other business entities whose primary purpose is to produce and release theatrical motion pictures. In a broader sense, the industry also includes film distributors, theater chains, merchandising subsidiaries, and such licensing and exhibition outlets as satellite, cable, Internet, and home video/DVD.

Feature films are the movies most commonly shown in large movie theaters. They typically last at least ninety minutes and tell a fictional story or a story based on real events but portrayed by actors. Large corporations, small companies, independent producers, government film boards, and even individuals are involved in the production of all kinds of films. Major Hollywood studios' are principally concerned with the marketable narrative feature. Most documentaries, low-budget features, and animated shorts, and avant-garde films are made outside the established industry.

Animated movies follow the same format as features, but use images created by artists. These films create the illusion of movement from a series of computer-generated images, two-dimensional drawings, or three-dimensional objects. Another form of film is the documentary, which deals primarily with fact, not fiction. Documentaries rarely appear in theaters, but they are seen regularly on satellite, cable and broadcast television. An experimental film is a sequence of images, abstract or literal, which do not necessarily form a narrative. An experimental film can be live action, animated, computer generated, or a combination of all three. Companies that wish to publicize their products or generate a favorable public image make industrial films. Educational films are specifically produced for viewing in classrooms. Their goal is to instruct, on subjects from science to first aid.

Film production is all the work that goes into the making of a movie, including its planning and realization. What is actually produced during this period is an approved, final version. All movies go through the following production stages: development, when the project is conceived, written, and financed; pre-production, when the shooting is prepared for; production, when the bulk of the script is staged, shot, and recorded; and post-production, when the picture and sound are edited and polished. During the distribution phase that follows production, the film is released, marketed, and exhibited.

Many different people contribute their skills and talents to the making of a film. Most of those who work on a production do not appear on camera. The key roles behind the scenes are the producer, director, screenwriter, unit production manager, casting director, director of photography, designers, assistant directors, sound and film editors, and music composer. The roles may differ or overlap depending on the individuals involved. The actors who appear on the screen are therefore only part of the story.

The producer is responsible for turning a movie idea into a successful picture. The producer must find money to pay for the production, hire actors and the production and technical teams, supervise the production process, and make arrangements for distributing the completed movie to theaters. If the producer has obtained financing from a studio or distributor, that organization may want a representative to be on hand during production. This person is referred to as the executive producer. Also, anyone who contributes time, effort, money, or influence to the motion picture, may be credited as associate producer.

Screenwriters develop original ideas or adapt previously written pieces of work as motion pictures. Adaptations may come from many sources including novels, short stories, lengthy poems, stage plays, comic books, magazine articles and musicals. Screenwriters can be commissioned to write a script for the screen or they can write a script on speculation or "on spec", meaning that the screenwriter is hoping that someone will purchase the rights to the independently written script and arrange it for production. Once a screenplay has been bought, the producer may choose to have it rewritten either by the original writer or by new writers.

Writing a script involves several steps. In addition to making up the story, the characters, and the dialogue, the writer's key contribution is to structure the narrative. The first step is to create an "outline," which is a short (one- or two-page) description of the action or plot. This is followed by a "treatment," which is a detailed description of the movie, containing a scene-by-scene story outline, some passages of dialogue and the subplots developed. Then the writer starts the full-length screenplay or script itself, which fills in all the details. It establishes the time and sets forth the place of the action, describes the characters' physical appearances, and supplies all the dialogue and action. Scripts also indicate where cameras are positioned and what camera movements occur while filming. Scripts indicate transition devices between scenes such as "dissolves" (when one image gradually replaces another), "fade-ins" (when an image gradually replaces the blank screen), "fade-outs" (when a blank screen gradually replaces the image), and straight "cuts" from one scene to the next.

Development begins when someone gets an idea for a movie. That person might be the head of a studio's story department, a producer who anticipates demand for a certain type of picture, or even a director. Most often, it is the writer. Legally, development begins when the producer hires a writer.

The script is then analyzed or "broken down" as to its production requirements. This important step determines how much each scene is liable to cost, what properties (props) and costumes will be necessary, and how efficiently the scenes may be arranged into an economical shooting schedule. It is normal for the scenes in a film to be shot in an order that is convenient rather than in the order of the script, a shooting method called "out of sequence". For example, all the scenes on a given set or location will most likely be shot at one time, no matter what the sequence.

Once the script has been written, researched for libel or other actionable qualities by in-house counsel, approved, and broken down and budgeted, and once financing has been secured, a commencement date is set. If the project is denied final approval it is offered to anyone who will reimburse the costs of development, a process called turnaround.

While the director is more responsible for the style of the movie, the writer is the one who determines the story to be told. The screenwriter has less creative autonomy than the director, however, and surrenders all control over the script when it is sold. The director is the person who oversees every aspect of film production. The director analyzes the script, visualizes how the picture should look, and guides the actors and the production crew as they execute that vision. The director is thus the coordinator of the entire production team and works closely with the actors on a day-to-day basis. The director is primarily responsible for the integration of camerawork, performance, and editing, and his/her creative control extends until the completion of the first edited version. When the film is ready to be edited, the director supervises the edited film or "first cut". The producers can re-edit the film, if they choose. Very few directors have the right to approve the final cut of a movie.

The unit production manager, or UPM, is responsible for scheduling, budgeting, selecting many of the crewmembers, and arranging for permits from various authorities and owners to shoot at locations outside the studio. The UPM, who reports directly to the producer, also oversees and supervises the purchase of goods and services, coordinates and handles the day-to-day business of running the production office, and ensures that the project stays within its budget.

The casting director selects actors and negotiates contracts during the hiring process, although when selecting stars for lead roles, the director and the producer usually make the final choice. When selecting actors for a film, casting directors take many factors into account, such as an actor's suitability for the role, name recognition and reputation, box-office appeal, acting ability, and experience.

The actors portray the variety of roles of the movie. To create believable characters, they rely on the details in the script, the director's vision, and their own interpretation of the role. A "day player" is an actor hired on a daily basis. This actor only has a few lines or scenes. The day player must be notified that they are finished by the end of the day; otherwise they are automatically called back for another day of work. People who appear in the background to lend reality to the film are not actors; they are called extras.

Many films involve physical movements or actions that could result in injury. These actions may be as dramatic as leaping off a moving train or as commonplace as bumping into a wall. During many potentially dangerous scenes, specially trained stuntmen and women fill in for the actors. This ensures that the stunt will be performed as safely as possible, and that the actors will not risk injury. Nevertheless, some actors insist on doing their own stunts, making producers worry about production insurance concerns and potential delays caused by injuries.

For scenes in which animals must perform, specially trained animal "actors" appear. These animals obey commands from their trainer while being filmed. Because of long hours of filming or because the animal grows or changes in appearance or in some other way during a filming schedule, multiple animals often appear in the same part.

The director of photography, also known as the DP or cinematographer, works with the director and interprets the action of the story using light, shade, composition, and camera movement. Other responsibilities include choosing the type of lens to be used for a shot, which influences the appearance of the image, and determining the camera's angle and position. The cinematographer rarely operates the camera directly; this function usually falls to a camera operator.

The production designer is responsible for the set designs, clothing, and the overall visual aspects or look of the movie. The production designer coordinates and supervises a team of specialized designers. The costume designer creates appropriate costumes or searches out vintage clothing in stores, specialized boutiques, or costume houses. Additional designers deal with makeup, lighting, and other visual aspects of the production. A "gaffer" supervises electrical work and is assisted by the "best boy." The "key grip" is responsible for the camera dolly (platform that supports and moves the camera) and all on-set logistical support, such as camera mounts, which are used to attach the camera to a vehicle or crane.

The assistant director or AD, assists the director in day-to-day tasks. On large productions, an AD may require the services of an assistant AD or second AD. The AD has many diverse duties, including creating the overall shooting schedule, which lists the days for filming each scene, and dealing with the problems that arise on the set. Each day the AD submits the following day's schedule for cast and crew, known as a "call sheet", to the UPM and the director for approval. The AD also works closely with the director during shooting, assisting in the preparation for each shot, getting the cast and crew to the right places at the right times, looking after extras, and taking care of many of the details involved in preparing for the next day's shooting.

A movie is filmed scene by scene, and a scene is filmed shot by shot. As mentioned, these scenes and shots are not usually filmed in the order that they appear in the film. This is because filming depends on factors such as actors' availability, weather conditions, script re-writes, and the set-construction schedule. Scenes that involve large, complicated sets that take longer to complete often are filmed near the end of the shooting schedule. A scene can be shot in a studio or "on location," meaning that it is filmed in a place that has not been specially constructed for the film.

Preparing for a film shot involves the supervision and coordination by the director of five main operations: The art department and props master prepare the set furnishings and the props the actors will use; the actors rehearse their lines and movements; the DP selects and arranges the lights; the camera operator rehearses the various camera movements and vantage points to be used in the shot; and the sound crew determines the placement of microphones and volume levels.

A "shot" is a continuously exposed piece of film, or the continuous view that is presented between one cut and another. A "take" is an attempt to photograph and/or record a particular shot. A specific shot is taken by one camera, equipped with one lens, from a particular camera setup or angle. In an edited film a scene will usually consist of more than one shot, and a full-fledged dramatic encounter in a given location may entail several different setups and as many shots as desired. A "sequence" is a consecutive series of shots and/or scenes, and it is not restricted to covering action in a single location. On the other hand, a sequence may also be any group of consecutive shots that relate significantly to each other, whether or not they are part of any scene. An entire scene could well be photographed from four or five camera setups and then edited into fifteen or more shots. One may not get a perfect shot on the first trial, or take. Each camera operator works from a list of camera positions, vantage points, and framing requirements for the full scene. Together the cameras cover all required angles. Using headsets to communicate with the camera operators, the director asks for camera adjustments during the filming of the scene and indicates to the technical director which cameras to use at each moment. The technical director ensures a master version of the selected shot is recorded.

Takes approved by the director are arranged into a final product that fulfills the vision of the producer and director. This responsibility falls to the editor. The editor first screens each day's film footage, called "dailies" or "rushes", for the director, producer, actors, and key members of the crew to view. Preparation of the dailies continues throughout the production period, meaning that the film is being edited at the same time that it is being shot. Screening the dailies allows the producer and director to choose the best shots and to decide if they need to re-shoot any scenes for artistic or technical reasons. After the principal filming is completed, the editor finishes the editing of the motion picture and supervises optical effects and titles that are to be inserted into the film.

The director, editor, or producer also may decide that sections of the film have inferior sound quality. In filmmaking, sounds are picked up by microphone and recorded digitally or on tape. During production a boom usually affixes or holds the microphone above the actors and out of camera range so that it is not visible on screen. Whenever possible, the original recording includes only dialogue because additional, peripheral sound can obscure the dialogue. Sometimes shooting outdoors results in too much unwanted noise, rendering some of the dialogue unusable. In this case, the actors later record replacement dialogue, and their lines are then synchronized with the picture. A sound editor re-records the actors' voices for these scenes. The actors speak the lines in the recording studio while viewing the scene on-screen. This process is called "looping" or "automatic dialogue replacement" (ADR). Sound editors also add recorded sound effects to complete a particular atmosphere or environment for the film. During postproduction, sound experts called Foley artists help create special sounds, including background or peripheral noises, in a recording studio. For instance, if a scene takes place in a park, the editors may add birds chirping and other appropriate background noises. One of the final steps in the editing process is the preparation and blending of the separate sound tracks (dialogue, music, sound effects) so that all the tracks are mixed together to create a cohesive, seamless unified sound experience for the viewing and listening audience.

The "production sound mixer" supervises the sound recording during a shoot. The "sound mixer" puts together all the sound for the final track by adjusting volume, fading noises in and out, and creating any other necessary audio effects. The music composer works with the director and editor to create a score that provides transitions between scenes and emotional ambience for the motion picture as a whole. Music is often used to underscore and enhance the dramatic content. The composer usually begins to score a picture only when it has reached the work-print stage. The composer works with the music editor, who prepares, times, and cuts the music track. The sound effects editor assembles all the sounds that are neither dialogue nor music. When all of the tracks have been edited and rerecorded, the final soundtrack is mixed in sync with the final work print.

Most film professionals, from sound engineers to set designers, work on a freelance basis, hired by a studio or by an independent producer for one project at a time. Agents have access to pools of talent they represent, including writers, directors, DPs, and performers.

Major Hollywood studios have vast resources and self-contained facilities that allow them to develop, produce, and release many pictures a year. Large studios contain a filming lot or location the size of a small town, including the studio office buildings, the script vaults, a film laboratory, thousands of costumes, standing outdoor sets, a lumberyard, prop-making shops, editing and mixing rooms, and a commissary or restaurant. They also maintain many windowless, soundproofed buildings lined up like huge concrete barns called sound stages, in which interior and some recreated exterior scenes are shot. The major studios often rent out their facilities to independent filmmakers and to those in the business of making movies for television. It is common for a major studio to participate in the financing of a picture or to buy it when it is completed, and then to release it under the studio logo. Thus a largely independent production, or even a foreign import, may well be released by one of the majors, even if it had little creative input. Nevertheless, most of the studios do release many of their own movies each year, and they usually control every element and aspect of those films.

A truly independent producer is one who finances and realizes a film without help from a major studio, and who is then free to license the motion pictures to an independent distributor. Many independent producers obtain financing by borrowing against pre-sold distribution rights, and by showing the script, budget, and proposed "talent package" (usually the director and the stars) to a bank, a loan institution, or a government film-financing department. An independent production usually costs much less than a studio production. That means the creators of an independent film can take creative risks and still earn a profit. Major studios usually back formula pictures rather than films that are artistically or socially provocative and challenging.

Most major and independent movies involve the same general filming process and technical aspects. A development stage precedes production. In this stage, the screenwriter writes the script and the producer hires the director and main actors, prepares a budget and shooting schedule, and raises the necessary money to pay for the production. The next stage, pre-production, involves the remaining preparatory work before production begins. During pre-production, the producer approves the final version of the script, the remaining cast and crew members are hired, and shooting locations are chosen. The director, assistant director, unit production manager, and producer plan the sequence for shooting the individual scenes. The producer, director, and designers work as a team to outline the visual look of the film. They plan how the scenes will be staged and finalize set construction, decoration, costumes, makeup and hair design, sound, and lighting.

As mentioned, pre-production is the period of converting the screenplay into a blueprint for the production of specific scenes; finding locations, hiring the cast, determining the shooting schedule, and fixing the final budget; designing and constructing the sets; making or buying the costumes and designing the makeup; researching to determine the accuracy of details; and working out the mechanical special effects staged before the camera, as opposed to optical special effects, which are done in the laboratory.

The essential collaboration during the development phase is between the writer and the producer. During pre-production the creative collaborators are the director, the designer, and the cinematographer. The first assistant director and the production manager, the producer's representative on the set, do the work of breaking down the script and drafting the shooting schedule.

The production designer integrates the sets, costumes, and color schemes into a comprehensive design. Although most of the creation of a soundtrack takes place in post-production, the sound design begins in pre-production. At this time, the cinematographer evaluates and tests how well the performers, sets, costumes and locations, will look on film.

When pre-production is completed, production can begin. Production is the period of principal photography of the scenes in the script that involve the principal actors. A second or third unit, each with its own director and crew, may shoot other scenes with crowds or stunt doubles, action sequences, or landscape shots. An insert unit shoots close-ups that are cut in, such as tight shots of maps, clocks, and other specific props. The technical aspects of the filming process include lighting the scene, operating the camera, and recording the sound.

Once the production stage has ended and the film has been shot, the project enters post-production. During this process, special effects can be added to the film to create dramatic visual images. Special optical effects add to the allure of movies. Filmmakers draw upon a variety of special effects to create illusions in the cinema. In digitization, images and sounds are stored as electronic files then viewed and edited on a computer. An independent unit makes optical special effects. The combining of picture elements is facilitated by computers, which are sometimes used to isolate and manipulate part or all of a frame that has been converted to digital information. Digitizing images allows them to be manipulated in almost any conceivable manner. The computer can also be used to generate its own images. The computer is widely used to control the repeated movements of certain special-effects cameras. Computer technology is utilized in the editing room to assemble a work print electronically, by choosing digital copies of shots and arranging them in a variety of trial sequences. Image programs allow for retouching damaged film, restoring classics movies, and adding electronic colors to black-and-white films.

After a movie has been shot, processed, edited, enhanced with special effects and sounds, mixed, and printed, it is ready to be distributed to individual theater chains and movie houses. This is accomplished through distributors, who lease films from the producer or production company. They arrange screenings so theaters can bid on the rights to show the film; promote and advertise the film; distribute or transmit copies of the film to the theaters; arrange for release on satellite, cable and broadcast television; coordinate distribution of videotapes, laser discs, and digital video discs to retailers; and keep detailed accounting records of the income and expenses for all aspects of film distribution. Upon receipt of attendance reports, distributors invoice theaters at the end of engagements. Sometimes films are not leased, but instead the producer subcontracts these distribution tasks to a distributor. The producer then pays for the services by giving the distributor a percentage of the film's net income. Additionally, the distributor deducts from the producer's share of the net profits the cost for supplying prints of the film and for marketing, advertising and promotion.

Many movies involve additional marketing beyond the movie itself. The movie's producers sometimes sell the rights to use the film's title, characters or images to various manufacturers. They produce and sell toys, games, clothing, and a wide variety of other products associated with the film. These ancillary or merchandising rights, along with the sale of musical recordings of the songs in the movie's sound track, generate huge revenues for the producers, as well as some star actors who also get a cut.

National rating associations rate movies to provide guidance to theater and home viewers about what kind of material the film is likely to contain. These rating systems guide parents as to which films are inappropriate or unsuitable for children under a certain age. Filtering technology helps parents automatically skip or mute sections of commercial movies on DVD. The manufacture and distribution of such electronic devices for DVD players is, however, controversial. The film's creators argue that changing the content – even when it is considered offensive – violates their copyrights. Studio executives feel they should be paid licensing fees for the alteration of their creative efforts. Some film companies prefer to control this process by producing edited DVD copies of popular movies and marketing them directly to consumers.

## TYPES OF MOTION PICTURES

**FEATURE**
**SHORT**
**ANIMATED**
**INDUSTRIAL**
**EXPERIMENTAL**
**DOCUMENTARY**
**EDUCATIONAL**
**POLITICAL**
**PROPAGANDA**

## FILM PRODUCTION STAGES

**DEVELOPMENT**
**PRE-PRODUCTION**
**PRODUCTION**
**POST-PRODUCTION**

## INDEPENDENT FILM FINANCING

**PRIVATE FUNDING**
**BANK - LOAN INSTITUTION**
**INTERNATIONAL CO-PRODUCTION**
**GOVERNMENT FILM-FINANCING PROGRAMS**
**BORROWING AGAINST PRE-SOLD DISTRIBUTION RIGHTS**

# KEY FILM PRODUCTION PERSONNEL

**PRODUCER / SCREENWRITER / DIRECTOR /
UNIT PRODUCTION MANAGER / CASTING DIRECTOR
/ ACTORS / DIRECTOR OF PHOTOGRAPHY (DP) /
DESIGNERS / ASSISTANT DIRECTORS /
FILM & SOUND EDITORS / MUSIC COMPOSER**

## SCREENPLAY ADAPTATION SOURCES

**NOVELS / SHORT STORIES / LENGTHY POEMS /
MAGAZINE ARTICLES / MUSICALS /
STAGE PLAYS / COMIC BOOKS**

## WRITING A MOVIE SCRIPT

**OUTLINE / TREATMENT / FULL-LENGTH SCREENPLAY
LEGAL LIABILITY VETTING / RE-WRITES**

## FIVE MAIN PRE-FILMING OPERATIONS

**PREPARATION OF SET FURNISHINGS & PROPS
ACTOR REHEARSALS
LIGHTING SET-UP
CAMERA POSITIONING
SOUND TESTS**

## FILMING PROCESS

**SCENE / SHOT / DAILIES or RUSHES / RE-SHOOT /
ROUGH EDITING / DIRECTOR'S CUT / FINAL CUT**

## COMMERCIALIZATION RIGHTS OF FILMS

**THEATRICAL DISTRIBUTION RIGHTS
TV RIGHTS
ANCILLARY/MERCHANDISING RIGHTS
REPRODUCTION RIGHTS (TAPE, DVD, INTERNET)**

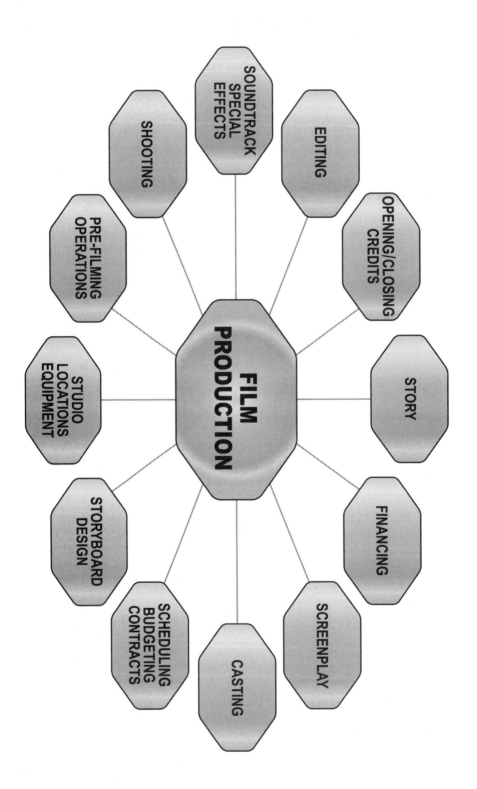

FILM PRODUCTION

- SOUNDTRACK SPECIAL EFFECTS
- SHOOTING
- PRE-FILMING OPERATIONS
- STUDIO LOCATIONS EQUIPMENT
- STORYBOARD DESIGN
- SCHEDULING BUDGETING CONTRACTS
- CASTING
- SCREENPLAY
- FINANCING
- STORY
- OPENING/CLOSING CREDITS
- EDITING

98

# FILM PRODUCTION "BEHIND THE SCENES" PERSONNEL

EXECUTIVE PRODUCER / PRODUCER
DIRECTOR / WRITER / CINEMATOGRAPHER
ART DIRECTOR / EDITOR / ASSOCIATE PRODUCER
STUNT COORDINATOR / PRODUCTION MANAGER
UNIT PRODUCTION MANAGER / LINE PRODUCER
ASSISTANT DIRECTOR / SECOND ASSISTANT DIRECTOR
CONTINUITY PERSON / CAMERA OPERATOR
ASSISTANT CAMERAMAN / FILM LOADER
STEAD CAM OPERATOR / PRODUCTION SOUND MIXER
FLOOR MANAGER / BOOM OPERATOR / GAFFER
KEY GRIP / DOLLY GRIP / RIGGER / RUNNER
BEST BOY / FOLEY ARTIST / AUDIO ENGINEER
ADR EDITOR / MUSIC MIXER / STILLS PHOTOGRAPHER
VISUAL EFFECTS DIRECTOR / FX COORDINATOR
POST-PRODUCTION SUPERVISOR / MATTE ARTIST
LOCATION SCOUTS / LOCATION MANAGER
PROPERTY MASTER / LEADMAN / SET DESIGNER
ELECTRICIAN / SET DRESSER / COSTUME DESIGNER
COSTUMER / MAKE-UP & PROSTHETICS ARTIST
BODY MAKE-UP ARTIST / HAIRDRESSER
DIALOGUE COACH / CHOREOGRAPHER
PRODUCTION OFFICE COORDINATOR
PRODUCTION ASSISTANT / UNIT PUBLICIST
SECOND UNIT DIRECTOR / PRODUCTION CATERER
CRAFT SERVICES / TRANSPORTATION COORDINATOR
NEGATIVE CUTTER / COLOR TIMER
DAY PLAYER / STAND-INS / BACKGROUND EXTRA
STORYBOARD ARTIST / STORY EDITOR
FASHION CONSULTANT / CASTING DIRECTOR
SINGING INSTRUCTOR / DANCE INSTRUCTOR
COPYRIGHT/TRADEMARK CLEARANCE COORDINATOR
FIGHT INSTRUCTOR / LIGHTING DIRECTOR
PUPPETEER / PERSONAL ASSISTANT / DRIVER
TRANSPORTATION, TRAVEL & LODGING COORDINATOR
HISTORIAN / LAWYER / ACCOUNTANT / BANKER

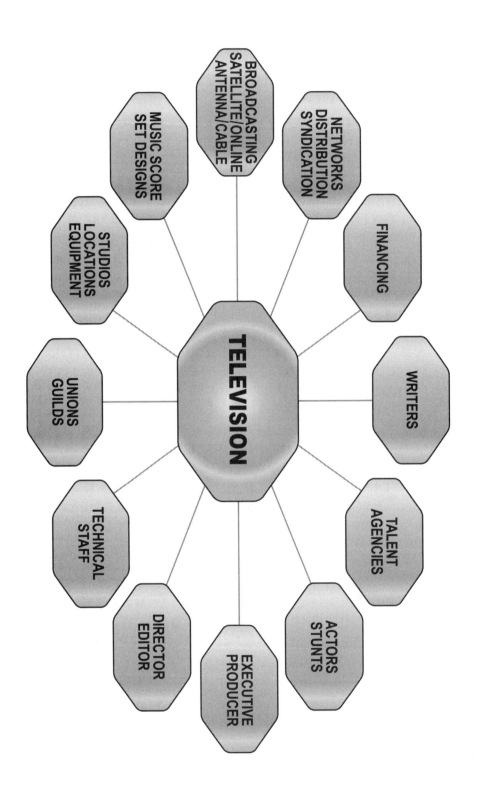

TELEVISION

- BROADCASTING SATELLITE/ONLINE ANTENNA/CABLE
- NETWORKS DISTRIBUTION SYNDICATION
- MUSIC SCORE SET DESIGNS
- FINANCING
- STUDIOS LOCATIONS EQUIPMENT
- WRITERS
- UNIONS GUILDS
- TALENT AGENCIES
- TECHNICAL STAFF
- ACTORS STUNTS
- DIRECTOR EDITOR
- EXECECUTIVE PRODUCER

# 7.   TELEVISION

The television industry is a business community of people and companies who create, control, disseminate, and broadcast television programming. This business community encompasses the writers, directors, producers, actors, and studio entities who create television entertainment; the television networks, broadcast/satellite/cable, that distribute programs; the syndicators who sell programs directly to local television stations; and the local private, public, and community run stations themselves. The television industry also includes the individual entrepreneurs and companies, both big and small, that own or are invested in television properties; advertisers or consultants who specialize in television technology or business practices; the reporters of the television trade press; the manufacturers of television sets and ancillary hardware; and the national government agencies or commissions that regulate TV and other electronic media.

The techniques used to create a television program are numerous and the entire process is complex. Most television programs are produced by production companies unrelated to the TV networks. These companies license their programs to the networks. The networks generate revenue by selling commercial time to sponsors.

Creating a television program typically involves developing a script, formulating a budget, designing a set, hiring a technical crew, and hiring creative talent and rehearsing lines before shooting starts. After filming, the post-production process includes video editing and the addition of sound, music, and visual effects. The three basic forms of TV programs are fictional, non-fictional, and live television. New program types are rarely introduced in broadcasting, since audience familiarity plays a vital role in determining programming. Fictional programs include daytime soap operas; situation comedies; dramatic series; movies made for television, including the multiple-part mini-series; some variety shows; and some children's programming. The basic non-fictional, or reality, programs include talk shows; game shows; religious programs; news; some children's programming; and magazine/informational shows that explore a variety of news stories in an entertainment format. Live television covers special events, sports, awards shows, telethons, news coverage, and talk shows.

The personnel involved in the production of a TV program include creative talent and technical crewmembers. The executive producer is responsible for the overall project and is usually the person who conceives the project and sells it to the network. The executive producer assumes final responsibility for the budget and all creative personnel, including the writer, director, producers, and the main actors. The writer(s) develop the script for each show. They often work during pre-production and rehearsals to fix problems encountered by the directors or actors, or to revise for artistic, budgetary or production considerations. The line producer reports to the executive producer and is responsible for the budget, crew, production logistics, and shooting schedule. Technical crewmembers include lighting, sound, electrical technicians, and camera operators.

Performers and actors are selected by the producer, and most audition to earn their part. Once they are hired, performers rehearse, while actors memorize their lines from a script and usually participate in a rehearsal before the program is shot. Performers may provide live commentary, or in the case of newscasters, they may read their lines from cue cards or a machine that displays words on a screen called a TelePrompTer.

The director helps select major cast members, locations, and the visual design of the production, such as the style of wardrobe and sets. Actors work under the direction of the director. In addition, the director is responsible for all camera angles and movements. After filming, the director and editor edit the videotape to create the director's cut.

The production manager is responsible for all physical production elements, including crew, equipment, and location. The assistant directors report to the director and are responsible for managing the extras, controlling the set, and carrying out the director's needs. The cinematographer, who operates the camera, is responsible for the movement of the camera and lighting the set. The production or art designer is responsible for the design, construction, and appearance of the sets and the wardrobe. The makeup artists and hair stylists usually report to the production designer. Videotape production involves a technical director, who is responsible for video recording. Video engineers are responsible for the quality and maintenance of the electronic equipment and their output. The key grip supervises the grips that set up and adjust production equipment on the set.

# MAIN STAGES OF TV SHOW PRODUCTION

## DEVELOPMENT
## PRE-PRODUCTION
## PRINCIPLE PHOTOGRAPHY
## POST-PRODUCTION

Producing a television show involves four main stages: development, pre-production, principle photography, and post-production.

The development of a television show starts with an idea or concept for a program and the creation of a script. Production companies or networks may require a commitment from key actors before financially committing to produce a show. Individual agents or talent agencies typically represent actors and performers. They receive a commission from the actor's remuneration. Various unions (representing actors, writers and creative/technical crews) guarantee minimum working and pay conditions.

Once the show has been developed, pre-production activities begin. Pre-production involves the planning, budgeting, and preparation required prior to the commencement of shooting. The pre-production period can last as long as a month or more for a film or mini-series, or just seven to ten days for a single episode of a dramatic/reality series or situation comedy (sit-com). Complex productions, such as a major sporting event or live-awards ceremony, may take months of pre-production.

The key people involved in pre-production are the production manager, director, and casting director. The production manager produces a preliminary budget, hires the location manager, finds crew department leaders, determines the location of shooting, and locks-in a start-of-production date. The director begins by reviewing the script for creative changes, selecting assistant directors and camera operators, and commences the casting process. Throughout the project, every decision involving cast, creative/technical crew, schedule, location, or visual components will require the director's input or approval. The pre-production process culminates with the final production meeting, attended by all producers and crewmembers, the writer(s), and the director. The pre-production team goes over the script in detail scene by scene. Each element of production is closely reviewed, while all questions and concerns are appropriately dealt with.

Following the pre-production stage the project enters into main production. Principle photography is the period in which television programs are shot. Scenes are scheduled to be shot according to production efficiency, not story progression. The program is assembled in sequential order during post-production. The result is a fully edited, complete show, requiring only music, visual/sound effects, and titles to be finalized.

Post-production begins with the completion of shooting and continues until the project is delivered to the television network for airing. The editing of filmed footage and the recording of a synchronized sound track are the main activities of post-production. Editing often begins during production. The director, producer, and network carefully review the footage from each day's shooting in the order in which it was shot. These dailies are then broken down and assembled into scenes by the editors. The first complete assemblage is shown to the director, who makes additional editing modifications and creates the director's cut. Thereafter, the producer and the network make additional modifications until a final cut is created. The final cut is given to the sound department, which is responsible for preparing the music tracks; sound effects; and dialogue tracks or recordings for final combination into one track. The final mixing of all the sound is called dubbing. During these dubbing sessions, the sound engineers will select or "spot" the points at which music will be inserted, and musicians will write and record the music. Sound effects are added, and sound engineers adjust dialogue recording for production quality and record new or replacement dialogue. The final stage of post-production is the addition of visual effects, such as scene fade-outs or dissolves, insertion of titles and credits; color correction; and creation of special optical effects including animations.

As entertainment audiences became more fragmented, and in order to remain profitable, television production and programming increasingly targets specific demographic groups and special interest viewers. Getting programming shown to the public can occur in many different ways. Following production the next step is to market and deliver the product to whatever markets are open to using it. First or original run showings happen when a producer creates a program of one or multiple episodes and shows it on a station or network that has either paid for the production itself or to which a license has been granted by the producers to do the same. Syndication is a term broadly used to describe secondary programming usages (beyond first run). It includes secondary runs in the country of first issue, but also international usage that may or may not be managed by the originating producer, who is also the copyright holder. Often the original producer chooses other individuals, companies, or stations to do the syndication work – in other words, to sell the product in the markets they are permitted to by contract.

Broadcasting is not the only effective means of delivering television programming to the general public. Other means of mass communication include: closed-circuit delivery systems, such as commercial cable television, pay-per-view, and modem-accessible databases, which transmit sounds and images to paid subscribers rather than to the general public; self-programmable systems, such as videocassette and digital recorders, the video game, and the CD-ROM, which allow the user more control over content and scheduling; and personal antennas capable of bypassing closed-circuit systems to capture satellite signals.

## BASIC FORMS OF TELEVISION PROGRAMS

### FICTIONAL / NON-FICTIONAL / LIVE

### CREATING A TELEVISION PROGRAM

**STORY OUTLINE**
**DEVELOPING A SCRIPT**
**FORMULATING A BUDGET**
**DESIGNING SETS**
**HIRING CREATIVE TALENT**
**HIRING TECHNICAL CREW**
**REHEARSING LINES/MOVEMENTS/STUNTS**
**SHOOTING – EDITING**
**ADDITION OF SOUND/VISUAL EFFECTS/THEME MUSIC**
**RECORDING OF A SYNCHRONIZED SOUND TRACK**
**CREDITS – FINAL CUT**

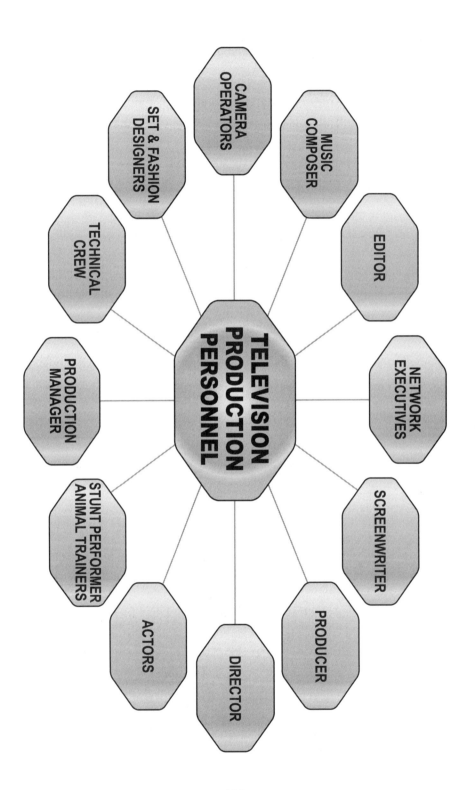

TELEVISION PRODUCTION PERSONNEL

- CAMERA OPERATORS
- SET & FASHION DESIGNERS
- MUSIC COMPOSER
- TECHNICAL CREW
- EDITOR
- PRODUCTION MANAGER
- NETWORK EXECUTIVES
- STUNT PERFORMER ANIMAL TRAINERS
- SCREENWRITER
- ACTORS
- DIRECTOR
- PRODUCER

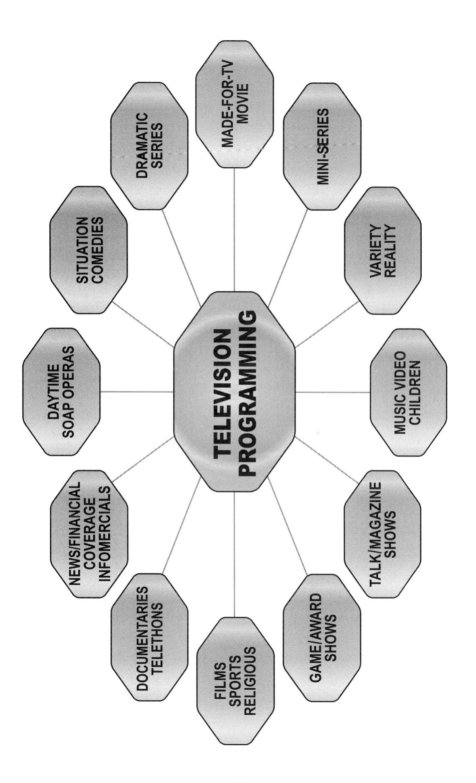

TELEVISION PROGRAMMING

- MADE-FOR-TV MOVIE
- DRAMATIC SERIES
- SITUATION COMEDIES
- DAYTIME SOAP OPERAS
- NEWS/FINANCIAL COVERAGE INFOMERCIALS
- DOCUMENTARIES TELETHONS
- FILMS SPORTS RELIGIOUS
- GAME/AWARD SHOWS
- TALK/MAGAZINE SHOWS
- MUSIC VIDEO CHILDREN
- VARIETY REALITY
- MINI-SERIES

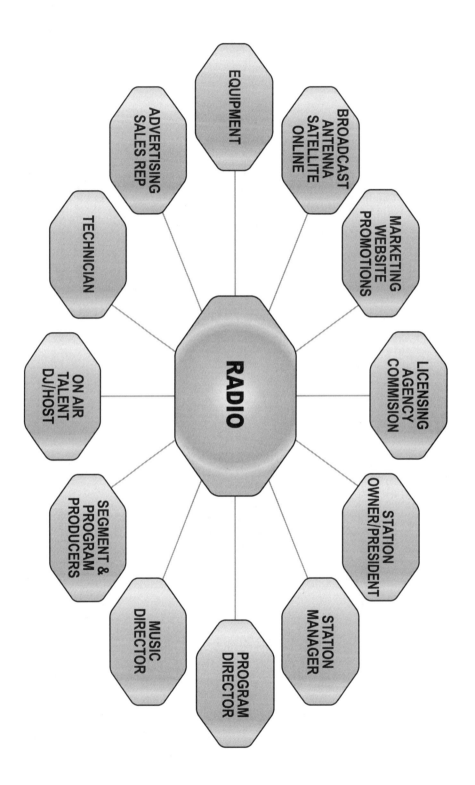

RADIO

EQUIPMENT

BROADCAST
ANTENNA
SATELLITE
ONLINE

ADVERTISING
SALES REP

MARKETING
WEBSITE
PROMOTIONS

TECHNICIAN

LICENSING
AGENCY
COMMISION

ON AIR
TALENT
DJ/HOST

STATION
OWNER/PRESIDENT

SEGMENT &
PROGRAM
PRODUCERS

STATION
MANAGER

MUSIC
DIRECTOR

PROGRAM
DIRECTOR

# 8.  RADIO

The radio industry is an important part of the overall entertainment business. It is a major form of entertainment and an influential force and conduit for promoting general entertainment products. Radio ads and talk radio programming help entertainment product sales (books, DVDs, video games etc.), while recorded music played on music stations helps stimulate record and concert ticket sales.

Generally speaking, radio is a form of communication in which sound is transmitted without wires from one point to another by means of electromagnetic waves. Radio requires no physical connection. It relies on the radiation of energy from a transmitting antenna in the form of radio waves. These radio waves, traveling at the speed of light, carry the information. When the waves arrive at a receiving antenna, a small electrical voltage is produced. After this voltage has been suitably amplified, the original information contained in the radio waves is retrieved and presented in an understandable form.

Although the method of detection differs in AM (amplitude modulation) and FM (frequency modulation) receivers, the same heterodyne principle is used in each. An FM receiver, however, generally includes automatic frequency control. Radio stations are almost evenly divided between AM and FM.

The prime advantage of FM, in addition to its fidelity, is its immunity to electrical noise, thereby offering a better quality sound that is more reliable. FM's superior audio is reflected in the music oriented programming adopted by the majority of its station. FM radio plays a major role in the introduction, growth, and dissemination of a variety of musical styles to a mass audience. Most FM stations are completely dedicated to the presentation of music. They tend to establish specific, easily identifiable music formats, such as popular music, jazz, country, rock, rap, R&B, or other genres that appeal to particular audiences. AM stations, on the other hand, are dominated by talk programming, including telephone call-up shows, all-news formats, political debate, newsmagazines, religious evangelism, and sports coverage.

Some of the most innovative work on radio today is heard on non-profit public, community, and college radio stations. Although new technologies have introduced additional competition to radio, they have also provided new outlets. Many radio shows are now simulcast on cable TV. In turn, television musical programming is also simulcast on radio. Many Internet services also carry radio programs to new audiences. Digital radio offers consumers a better reception and sound quality than the traditional analogue technology. Some digital stations are not advertisement driven like most conventional stations – avoiding ads in lieu of paid client subscriptions.

Primarily because broadcasting signals move through the air without regard to political borders, federal/national government communications commissions or independent government agencies retain oversight of broadcasting. They oversee the regulating and licensing of radio stations and radio operators. In order to broadcast, a radio operator's permit or radio license is needed. This certificate grants permission to an individual or company to transmit radio broadcasts. The broad responsibilities of these independent government agencies include the licensing and regulation of television broadcasters and the oversight of other communications technologies, including telephone, Internet, cable TV and satellite transmission. All radio and TV station licenses are subject to periodic renewal by these commissions, as is the transfer of any of these licenses from one owner to another by sale or merger. While the agencies are concerned with broad policy issues, such as mature subject matter in program content, they also have oversight of technical standards for the introduction of industry advances. The Internet, due to its borderless and international nature, presents unique challenges for agencies such as the Federal Communications Commissions (FCC) in the United States and the Canadian Radio-television and Telecommunications Commission (CRTC) in Canada.

North American radio and TV stations fall into one of four generic categories: "owned and operated," which are properties held directly by the networks; "affiliates," which are owned by other companies that contract for exclusive rights to carry the programming of a particular network in a given market; "independents," commercial stations that do not contract for rights to carry network programming; and "non-profits", public/college/community stations that do not carry commercial network programming and operate on contributions from viewers, foundation grants, corporate gifts, and production support from various levels of government.

Advertising agencies purchase airtime and place ads with both local and national network radio shows. Stations sometime sell agencies full sponsorship, which includes placing the product name in a show's title. The fee charged for advertisements is based on the audience size and demographics of stations and their particular shows. As is the case with television, ratings service companies survey radio audience size by employing various methods to sample listener profiles and record their program choices. The size of any given program's audience is then estimated, based on the reactions of these sample viewers The resulting projections, or ratings, determine the price of ads during the program and, ultimately, whether the program will remain on the air or eventually face cancellation.

New broadcast delivery systems continue to be developed. For example, Direct Broadcast Satellite (DBS) provides the radio listener with a personal antenna capable of bypassing closed-circuit systems to capture satellite signals. However, most of the channels available from satellites require subscription fees and licenses, making DBS a form of "narrow-casting" (transmission to a specific group rather than to the general public). Podcasting is a method of publishing files via the Internet, allowing users to subscribe to a feed to receive new files automatically. It is popular for downloading audio files onto a portable audio player or personal computer and has become a new outlet for commercial and public radio stations.

A radio format or programming format describes the overall content broadcast on a radio station. Radio formats are frequently employed as a marketing tool, and constantly evolve. Music radio; news radio; sports radio; talk radio; and weather radio describe the operation of different genres of radio format and each format can often be sub-divided into many specialty formats. For example, the following sub-list of broadcasting station categories employs singular or combination radio formats and are further defined in application by the market that they serve: college radio, commercial radio, community radio, public radio, pirate radio, closed circuit radio.

Although the methods by which listeners tune into radio programs are constantly evolving, as an entertainment medium radio remains profitable, vibrant, and effective.

# RADIO FORMATS

Active rock – Adult contemporary (AC) – Adult standards/Middle of the road (MOR) – Adult album alternative (Adult alternative/AAA) – Adult oriented rock (Album oriented rock/AOR) – Alternative rock (Alternative) – Beautiful music – Big band – Black gospel – Blues – Canto-pop (Cantonese pop music) – Caribbean (reggae, soca, merengue, cumbia, salsa) – Children's radio – Christian Contemporary – Classic country – Classic hits – Classic rock – Classical – College radio – Comedy - Contemporary inspirational - Contemporary hit radio (CHR) – Country – Dance – Easy listening – Educational – 50s/60s/70s/80s/90s Hits – Electronica – Ethnic – European Hit Radio (EHR) – Evangelical Christian – Financial News – Freeform (Disc jockey-selected) – General service – Gospel – Hard Rock – Health/Leisure – Hindi film music – History – Hot adult contemporary (Hot AC) – Hot hits (Hot 100/Top 40/Top 30/Top 20/Top 10 – Hurban/CHR (bilingual Hispanic youth format) – Jazz – Mainstream rock – Metal (Heavy/Thrash/Speed Metal) – Modern adult contemporary (Modern AC) – Modern rock – Music radio – New adult contemporary/Smooth Jazz (New AC) – New country/Young country – News radio – Nostalgia – Oldies (Golden Oldies) – Polka – Politics – Pop Standards – R&B (rhythm and blues) – Radio documentary – Ranchera – Rap/Hip-hop – Regional Mexican (banda, corridos, ranchera, conjunto, mariachi, norteño, etc.) – Religious – Rhythmic – Rock – Soft adult contemporary (Soft AC) – Soft rock – Soul music – Sports (Sports/Talk) – Talk radio (News/Talk) – Tejano (Texas/Mexican music) – Traffic  – Travel – Tourism Tropical (salsa, merengue, cumbia) – Urban contemporary (black rap, hip-hop, soul, R&B) – Urban adult contemporary (Urban AC, black R&B, soul, gospel) – Urban oldies – Variety – Weather – World beat – World/International/Global headlines – World music

## GENERIC CATEGORIES OF RADIO STATIONS

### OWNED AND OPERATED / AFFILIATES
### INDEPENDENTS / NON-PROFIT

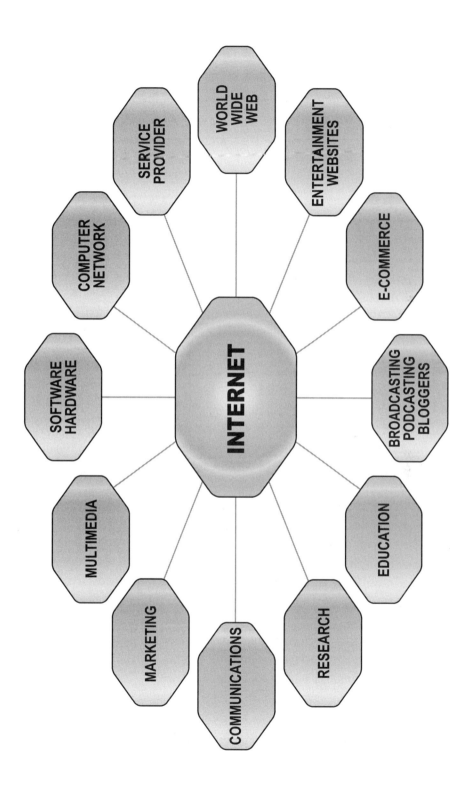

INTERNET

WORLD WIDE WEB
SERVICE PROVIDER
ENTERTAINMENT WEBSITES
COMPUTER NETWORK
E-COMMERCE
SOFTWARE HARDWARE
BROADCASTING PODCASTING BLOGGERS
MULTIMEDIA
EDUCATION
MARKETING
RESEARCH
COMMUNICATIONS

# 9.   INTERNET


The Internet is an international computer network linking together thousands of individual networks at government and military agencies, educational institutions, nonprofit organizations, financial and industrial corporations of all sizes, and commercial enterprises (called service providers or gateways) that enable people around the world to access the network. An individual at a computer terminal or personal computer (PC) with the proper computer software communicates across the Internet by placing data in an electronic Internet Protocol (IP) packet and addressing it to a particular destination on the Internet. Communications software on the intervening networks read the addresses and forwards the packets.

A 32-bit binary number called an IP address uniquely identifies each computer that is directly connected to the Internet. This address is usually seen as a four-part decimal number, each part equating to 8 bits of the 32-bit address in the decimal range 0–255. Because an address of the form 4.33.222.111 could be difficult to remember, a system of Internet addresses, or domain names, was developed. Reading from left to right, the parts of a domain name go from specific to general. The rightmost part, or top-level domain/suffix/zone, can be a two-letter abbreviation of the country in which the computer is in operation. Hundreds of abbreviations, such as "us" for United States and "ca" for Canada, have been assigned. It is common for a site to use a specialized top-level domain such as "gov" (government) or "edu" (educational institution) or one of the four domains designated for open registration worldwide, "com" (commercial), "org" (organization), "net" (network), or "int" (international). A domain-name server (an Internet-connected computer running a database program) translates an Internet address into an IP address.

The Internet, or simply the Net, is a publicly available computer-based worldwide information network composed of a large number of smaller interconnected networks called internets. These internets may connect many computers, enabling them to share information with each other and to share various resources, such as powerful supercomputers and databases of information. This international web of interconnected networks makes it possible for individuals, organizations, and businesses

114

to effectively and inexpensively communicate with each other.

The public information stored in the multitude of computer networks connected to the Internet forms a huge electronic library, but the enormous quantity of data and number of linked computer networks also make it difficult to find where the desired information resides and then to retrieve it. A number of progressively easier-to-use interfaces and tools exist to facilitate searching. Among these are powerful search engines and a number of commercial indexes.

The internets from which the Internet is composed are usually public access networks (Local Area Network or LAN; Wide Area Network), meaning that the resources of the network can be shared with anyone logging on to, or accessing, the network. The File Transfer Protocol (FTP) is used to transfer information between computers in different networks, thus allowing users of one computer to connect with another distant computer in a different network. Other types of internets, called intranets, are closed to public use. Intranets are the most common type of computer network used in organizations and businesses where it is important to restrict access to the information contained on the network.

Unlike traditional broadcasting media, such as television and radio, the Internet is a decentralized system. Each connected individual can communicate with anyone else on the Internet, can publish ideas, and can sell products with a minimum overhead cost. The Internet dramatically impacts education and business as entertainment companies offer goods and services online.

The Internet began in the late 1960s as a communication and research tool used almost exclusively for academic and military purposes. This changed in 1989 with the introduction of the World Wide Web (also referred to as W3 or WWW) – a system that makes browsing the Internet both fast and intuitive. The WWW is a set of programs, standards, and protocols governing the way in which multimedia files (documents that may contain graphics, text, photographs, audio, and video) are created and displayed on the Internet. The Internet contains the WWW and also includes all the hardware (computers, supercomputers, connections) and non-WWW software and protocols on which the WWW runs. The difference between the Internet and the WWW is similar to the distinction between a computer and a multimedia program that runs on the computer.

Artists, entertainment companies and institutions use the

Internet in many ways. Companies use the Internet to provide access to complex databases, such as financial databases. Businesses can carry out commerce online (e-commerce), including advertising, selling, buying, distributing products, and providing after-sales services. Businesses and institutions can use the Internet for voice and video conferencing and other forms of communication that allow people to telecommute, or work from a distance. The use of electronic mail or e-mail over the Internet quickens communication between businesses, among employees, and between other individuals. Media and entertainment companies use the Internet to broadcast video and audio, including live television and radio programs; to offer online chat, in which people carry on discussions using written text; and to offer online news, information, and weather programs. Scholars, researchers, and scientists use the Internet to communicate with colleagues and co-workers, to distribute lecture notes and course materials to students, to conduct research, and to publish data, papers, and articles. Individuals use the Internet for communication, entertainment, finding information, and to buy and sell goods and services.

The popularity of the Internet, however, is a double-edged sword for the entertainment industry. Due to the graphics-intensive nature of the World Wide Web, images, as well as sound, can be transferred, exchanged, and downloaded without proper authorization from the owners of these materials. Copyright infringement occurs mainly through peer-to-peer file-swapping or file-sharing software, but also through private members-only chat rooms, or even the sale of counterfeit artwork, CDs, DVDs and software masquerading as legitimate product.

Piracy of intellectual property and cultural products can be identified. As mentioned, the IP address is a numeric code used to identify a computer when transmitting information on the Net. Internet companies use the figure to pinpoint the computer sending or receiving illegal material. Legislators are faced with the delicate task of clarifying liability for Internet service providers, while facilitating the use of the Internet for legitimate educational and research purposes. Some courts have ruled that Internet service providers do not have to pay tariffs or royalties to music artists simply because they provide the technology to access downloading or "swapping" sites; implying that artists should ask for royalties from individual sites that offer their works.

Electronic copying sold over the Internet is high-tech digital piracy. This is not a victimless crime. The people who create and publish these works are being robbed of literally millions of dollars, and owners are now sending a clear message that they can and will take action to prevent this kind of copyright infringement. Similar to the music industry's response to file-sharing service sites and the illicit copying of music, the movie industry is also aggressively pursuing violators. Copyright protection online, illegal copying, and appropriate compensation for creators and owners are serious Internet issues that present important challenges to the entertainment industry at large.

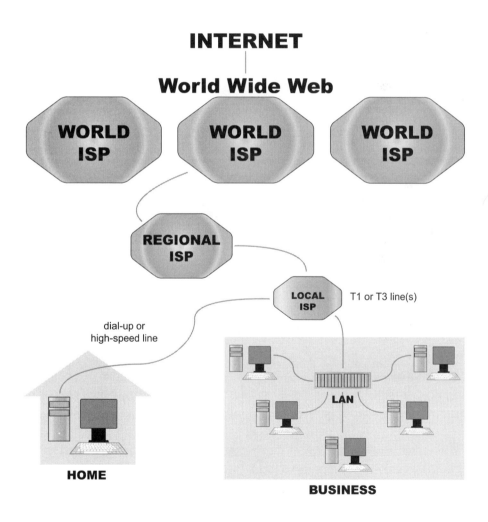

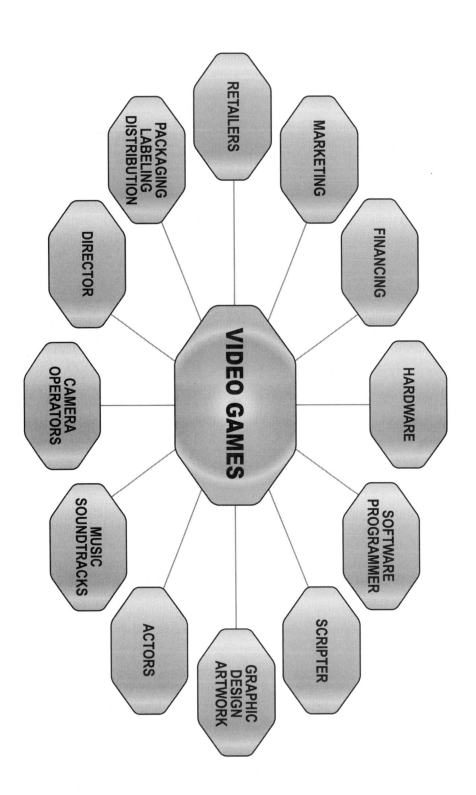

VIDEO GAMES

RETAILERS

MARKETING

PACKAGING LABELING DISTRIBUTION

FINANCING

DIRECTOR

HARDWARE

CAMERA OPERATORS

SOFTWARE PROGRAMMER

MUSIC SOUNDTRACKS

SCRIPTER

ACTORS

GRAPHIC DESIGN ARTWORK

118

# 10. VIDEO GAMES

Video games, often referred to as computer or electronic games, are computer programs that use a combination of text, computer graphics, video, and sound to create action, or game play. They range from simple games for kids to realistic and sophisticated games suitable for training aviators, train conductors, and ship captains. In each case, the player controls the action by means of an input device, such as the buttons on a mouse or a joystick.

A player may be the game's sole protagonist, navigating through a web of possible actions, interacting with the game's moves, and winning through a combination of knowledge, dexterity, and strategy. In other cases, players compete not against the program but against one or more other individuals, who may input their moves into the same machine or into computers at other locations around the world that communicate via computer networks. The Internet provides web games and international gaming, complete with on-line gaming leagues in which players from around the world compete against one another in tournaments. Some on-line gaming services are free of charge, while others are pay-to-play.

Many games are written, tested, and designed to be played on personal computers. Others are designed for arcade or hand-held game machines, or home video game consoles that plug into a screen monitor or television set. Frequently, different versions of the same game are available for a number of these platforms, since each platform has certain advantages and disadvantages.

An arcade machine allows one or more people to play a game for a set number of minutes after inserting a coin. A typical arcade machine is dedicated to a specific game. For example, an arcade machine may offer a hunting game that is the only computer software in the machine; even the hardware is especially designed for that game, including controllers that are mounted on a gun rather than on a standard joystick. Arcade games generally require good hand-eye coordination and have several levels of complexity and speed. Some have pinball-type action, while others send players through complicated mazes.

Mobile or hand-held game machines are small, inexpensive units that use interchangeable cartridges, much like the larger console systems, or game programs downloaded via the Internet. Other hand-helds have specific games built into them during the manufacturing progress. Home video-game consoles are specifically engineered to play games. All consoles of a specific brand model are alike, and the consoles are self-contained units that are not changed by the owners. Game designers can create a game knowing that everyone who is going to purchase the game has the exact same piece of hardware, even though it may not contain the latest technological accessories.

Personal computers have more memory and power than game consoles, allowing designers to create more imaginative and challenging games. PCs constantly change as new hardware becomes available. A consumer who purchased a computer one year, however, may upgrade it the next year with a new video card or a faster processor. Since not everyone who owns a PC has the latest technology, game designers determine an acceptable level of minimal system requirements. Many consumers regularly upgrade their existing machines or purchase newer models in order to maintain optimum gaming performance. Indeed, entertainment software not only is the major force driving sales of home PCs, it is also an indicator of where PC technology is heading.

The evolution of video games, like the evolution of computers, has been one of trickle-down technology, in which advancements introduced on supercomputers and mainframe computers gradually make their way down to consumer devices. Game designers constantly strive to squeeze more power and memory into less space, improve the realistic look of games, and make them play faster. Computer games offer consumers rich color palettes, realistic sounds, quick re-drawings, diverse camera angles, great intuitive play and complexity. Imaginative programmers offer an almost limitless array of exotic worlds, stimulating adventures and fantastic situations.

Many video games are models of real-life situations in which, unlike real life, the issues are quite simply drawn and the players can become engaged without all the confusions that surround everyday action, commitments and decision-making. The basic function of games is to intensify human experience in ways that are relatively safe, even while they provide suspense, passion and excitement. Typically, games simulate the more intense human experiences: intellectual contest, physical combat, and the expectancy and excitement involved in random, unpredictable occurrences.

Although many thousands of game titles are available on the market, the vast majority fall into one of several categories or are hybrids that blend or extract aspects of various categories. The main categories are: children's games; traditional board/word/card games; skill and simulation games that recreate real-life situations and sports; games of strategy, in which the player must analyze a situation, understand or discover the rules that govern the situation, and plan a strategy to achieve success; fantasy and adventure games that emphasize character and plot; games of chance; and, games based on popular films/books/TV shows, allowing players to choose among various scenarios and outcomes. Although many games incorporate educational content, the best-selling video games usually contain objectionable values implicit in the games; particularly those games that involve extremely violent or aberrant situations, events, and characters, including those that reward players for making a kill. As is the case with most entertainment, appropriate content in electronic games is subjective, and therefore controversial.

Video games offer an alternative medium to ad agencies, as their corporate clients court consumers who have cut back on commercial radio listening and television viewing. Advertising within video games allows marketers direct access to target demographics, while helping video game companies meet rising development and production costs. Only about ten percent of video games become popular enough to make money. The ad industry holds out video-game advertising as a way to reach young men ages 18 to 34, a coveted demographic that is slipping away from the grasp of traditional media. Advertisers can create a game around a product (known as "advergaming") rather than place their brands within a well-known title. Blue-chip advertisers have signed on to this new approach, with ads appearing within the virtual game landscape as billboards, vending machines or store windows. Video-game advertising also gets a boost from technologies that help target individual consumers better and rotate advertising messages more easily; as well as the rise of games played on shared networks like the Internet or wireless devices.

The video game industry is a major component of the worldwide entertainment industry, generating annual revenues in North America that are approximately double those claimed by the film industry. With the convergence of music, video, communication, wireless networking, and game functionality, the video game industry employs the services, talent, and creativity of a cross-section of the entertainment industry's labor force. For example, many popular video games feature live action actors with original dialogue and music – the ultimate fusion of entertainment mediums, bringing together music, video, gaming and storytelling. Film directors, scriptwriters, costume/set designers, and technical crews are also participating. Professional talent from other entertainment fields are thus benefiting directly from the enormous worldwide success and expansion of the video game industry.

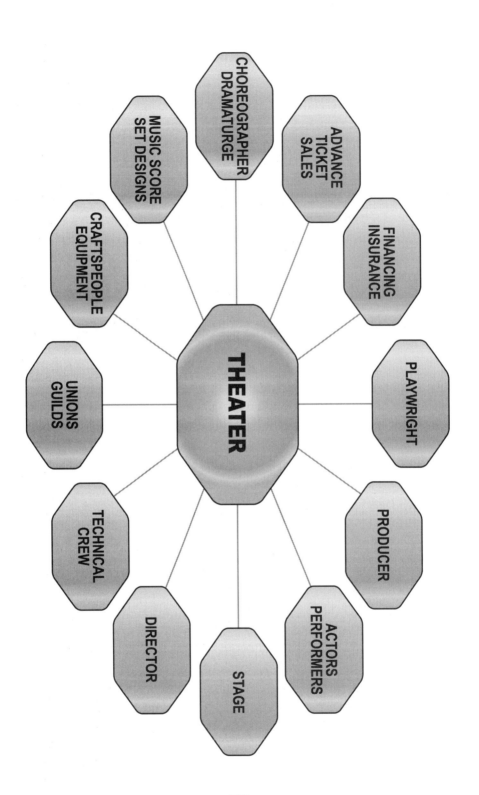

THEATER

- CHOREOGRAPHER DRAMATURGE
- MUSIC SCORE SET DESIGNS
- CRAFTSPEOPLE EQUIPMENT
- UNIONS GUILDS
- TECHNICAL CREW
- DIRECTOR
- STAGE
- ACTORS PERFORMERS
- PRODUCER
- PLAYWRIGHT
- FINANCING INSURANCE
- ADVANCE TICKET SALES

# 11. THEATER

Theater is one of the long-standing and most popular forms of entertainment. Theater takes place when entertainers or actors perform live for an audience on a stage or in a space designated for the performance. The space set aside for performances, either temporarily or permanently, is also known as a theater. In this empty space entertainers perform or actors present themselves in a story about some aspect of human experience. The actors, the audience, the space, and the performance are the essentials of theater. Theater performances include puppet shows, vaudeville, pantomime, circus, and other forms of entertainment; however, the performance is very often a play – comedy, tragedy, or musical.

The word "theater" comes from the Greek word "theatron", meaning "seeing place." Actors and performers use a variety of locations for theater, including churches, amphitheaters, parks, marketplaces, restaurants, basements, tents, garages, warehouses, nightclubs, street corners, and community halls. It is not the building that makes theater but rather the use of space by actors and performers. In addition to the actor and the audience in a space, a written or improvised story is often needed. Sometimes referred to as "drama," the playwright's theatrical texts usually provide the fundamentals of a performance.

Theatrical performances require the collaborative efforts of many creative people, including artists, craftspeople, technician crews, entrepreneurs, and managers. Theater is thus a diverse and complex art and business. Theatrical events include such production elements as costumes, scenery, props, lighting, sound, music, and choreography. Each element in theater has its own composer, choreographer, or designer, who collaborates with the director to focus the audience's attention on the performers and action.

Organizations that produce theater or theater companies range from commercial theaters on Broadway in New York City or the West End in London, to nonprofit resident companies subsidized by boards of directors, corporations, government agencies, and charitable foundations. Commercial producers organize single productions for the purpose of staging the work and making money for investors. Educational and amateur theaters organize their efforts in ways similar to commercial theaters. Resident theater companies, which generally are nonprofit organizations, stage a wide variety of works. Resident groups, composed of actors, directors, playwrights, craftspeople, designers, and managers, are subsidized through the theater's box office, government grants, and contributions from foundations, businesses and individuals. Unlike commercial theaters, which specialize in one production at a time, resident companies usually produce a season of plays in sequence, or several plays in repertory that are rotated over a period of time. Some resident companies are built around the artistic vision of a particular director.

All theaters require creative, managerial, and technical people as part of a permanent staff to prepare and offer productions on a scheduled basis. The administrative staff includes the producer, casting director, publicist, box-office personnel, house managers, and ushers. The technical staff includes the production manager, technical director, stage manager, construction staff (scenery, props, costumes), electrical and sound technicians, and running crews. In general, the creative staff consists of a director, actors, and designers. Sometimes, when necessary and affordable, a playwright, choreographer, composer, musical director, voice and dialect coach, stunt or fight director, and literary manager or "dramaturge," are added to the staff. In smaller nonprofit, community, or educational theaters, personnel may assume responsibility for several positions or duties. Generally, commercial and noncommercial production teams vary only in complexity, range and size.

Producing a musical requires a musical director and a choreographer. The musical director oversees the performances of the on-stage singers and musicians, as well as the off-stage orchestra. The choreographer is responsible for hiring dancers and preparing dance numbers. The voice and dialect coach, the stunt or fight director, and dramaturge, have also become indispensable members of many theater companies. The voice and dialect coach advises actors on diction, audibility, and comprehension, while the stunt or fight director ensures the actors' safety by choreographing and rehearsing any risky action, movements or fight scenes. The dramaturge works with the director to select and prepare scripts for performance, advises the director and actors on the details of the play's background, history and interpretation, and prepares material such as program notes to help the audience better appreciate and fully enjoy the play.

In commercial and nonprofit theaters, the producer is the person who puts together the financing, management staff, and the artistic team to mount the show. This framework helps dictate the overall artistic effect of the production. In nonprofit companies, the producer is often the group's artistic director who selects a season of several plays, hires the artistic talent and technical crew, collaborates with a casting director to audition and cast actors in the various parts, controls the theater's funding, and acts as the final decision-maker in all administrative and artistic operations.

The commercial producer, with the help of assistants, licenses a playwright's script, raises funds from investors, "angels," or "backers," hires the artistic staff, negotiates with unions, rents a theater and theatrical equipment, supervises publicity and ticket sales, and takes responsibility for all insurance and financial aspects of the production. Several producers are often needed to acquire the funding needed to produce a large musical on Broadway. Usually, the producer works together with a general manager and others to accomplish the daily running of the production, from rehearsals to closing. The producer also oversees the sale of subsidiary rights to touring companies and the recording industry, or for motion picture or TV adaptations and broadcasts.

Directors assume responsibility for the overall interpretation of a script, and they have the authority to approve, guide and coordinate all the aspects of a production. They control all artistic or creative elements of a production, dictate financial matters, and make decisions on casting, costumes, and scenery. The role of the director is to create a unified, harmonious artistic product on stage, and be responsible for all creative decisions. The stage director collaborates with the playwright, actors, designers, and technicians to stage a carefully crafted vision of life based upon a personal interpretation of the script.

Theatrical stage performers are puppeteers, jugglers, minstrels, pantomimes, magicians, acrobats, clowns, ventriloquists, dancers, singers, musicians, and amateur/professional actors. The actor is the creative artist most identified by audiences with their experience of theater. Acting begins with an individual's talent, discipline, imagination, the need to express, and the process of observation. Through years of training with experienced coaches, learned technique and long rehearsals, the actor is able to convey the emotional and psychological truth of the character's behavior within the context of the play. Most professional stage actors in North America are members of unions, guilds, or associations. The majority of professional acting jobs are found in regional theaters located across the continent. Most union actors have an agent to represent them. Agents work through casting directors, who seek actors for auditions in order to cast them in productions or invite them to join touring or permanent theatrical companies. The casting director is employed by the producer to assist in arranging casting sessions. In these sessions, agents send professional actors to audition for roles.

Designers work in tandem with directors to create an environment for a play. The designers' work is to shape and fill the stage space and to make the play visibly stimulating and interesting. There are four main types of designers: scene, costume, lighting, and sound.

Various artists are responsible for different design effects. The scene designer, also called the scenic or set designer, provides realistic settings, props, and furniture to make the stage appear like the play's actual setting. The costume designer is the creative artist responsible for how the characters look. Costume design includes a character's garments, accessories, hairstyle or wig, makeup, and masks. As a design element, costumes help establish a character's social class, economic status, sex, age, and occupation. They can also assist in identifying a play's era, geographic location, weather, and time of day. The complex demands of stage production required specialized, trained costume designers to meticulously design, choose, and control the elements of clothing as they relate to the total production design. Like the scene designer, costume designer's work to supplement the director's understanding of the play and the characters' lives visually through clothing, paying close attention to fabric, texture, color, and style. In the commercial theater, costume designers have their own design studios and utilize construction shops with cutters, drapers, and sewing professionals or "stitchers" to execute their designs.

Makeup enhances an actor's visibility and makes facial features distinctive. Like a costume, it helps an actor reveal character by giving physical clues to personality, age, sex, race, background, health, and environment. Basic stage makeup, consisting of foundation and color shadings, is used to prevent the actor from appearing pale or washed out beneath powerful stage lights. Wigs are designed by a wig specialist and are used to lend authenticity to plays set in historical periods or to alter entirely the actor's normal appearance. Masks enlarge the actor's features for visibility at great distances, and they help portray and express basic human emotions. Effective masks are comfortable, lightweight, and molded to the contours of the actor's face. The costume designer has final approval of the actor's mask, makeup, wigs, and hair.

The lighting designer uses light as an artistic medium in the theater. Stage lighting affects what audiences see. Properly planned lighting can control the audience's focus of attention, and enhance the meaning of the play. The ability to control lighting effects make it possible to include a range of colors and intensities, establish mood, create atmosphere, and highlight areas of the stage. Lighting designers use a variety of sophisticated equipment, such as computerized light boards, to achieve the desired effects. Like the theater's other designers, lighting designers work with the director and other designers to achieve a cohesive, seamless production.

The director's creative team also includes the sound designer. The technological capability for both live and recorded sound provides the director with an endless variety of nature, location, and abstract sounds to highlight moods. Collaborating with the director, the sound designer identifies the effects required by the script and adds a creative element to enhance atmosphere. State of the art sound technology is usually available to commercial production sound designers.

Theater is designed to entertain, motivate, persuade, instruct, and shock. But whatever the intentions of the director, performers, and creative/technical crews, the final result depends on the interaction with an audience. Some audiences want only to be entertained. Others want the theater to provide new understanding and insight about historical, social, political, or personal issues. Ultimately, audiences vote through their attendance or nonattendance. They support what appeals to them and generally abandon or ignore what they find unpleasant, offensive, or incomprehensible. As is the case with all entertainment industries, it is the marketplace that ultimately rules the theater industry.


## FOUR MAIN TYPES OF THEATER DESIGNERS


**SCENE**
**COSTUME**
**LIGHTING**
**SOUND**

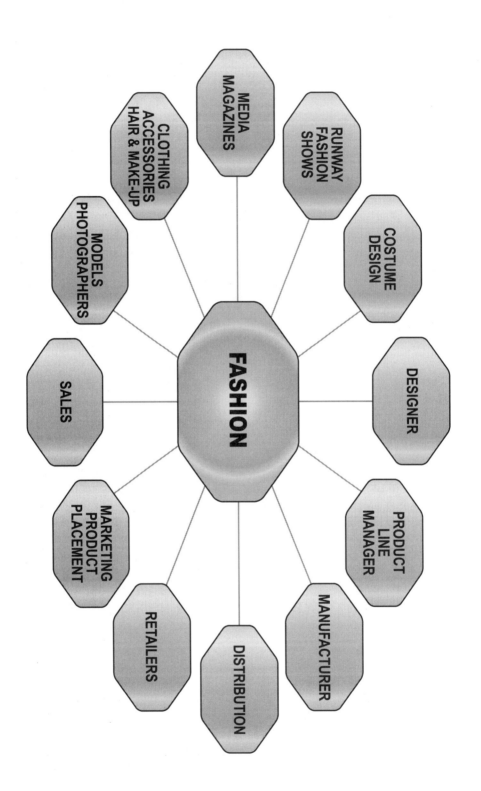

FASHION

MEDIA MAGAZINES

RUNWAY FASHION SHOWS

CLOTHING ACCESSORIES HAIR & MAKE-UP

COSTUME DESIGN

MODELS PHOTOGRAPHERS

DESIGNER

SALES

PRODUCT LINE MANAGER

MARKETING PRODUCT PLACEMENT

MANUFACTURER

RETAILERS

DISTRIBUTION

# 12.  FASHION

Fashion is an integral part of pop culture and the entertainment industry. The term "fashion" applies to clothing, garments or dress, and refers to trends, modes, fads or styles that are popular at any particular time. In a broader sense, fashion can also include jewelry, hair & make-up, clothing accessories, and even tattoos or piercings. Show business factors that impinge on fashion are manifold, ranging from impressive cultural events (award shows, premieres, galas) to the popularity of celebrities. The influence of clothing designers and major fashion houses that constitute the high-quality design and dressmaking or "haute couture" are a decisive factor in North American and European fashion. However, Prêt-à-Porter or ready-to-wear collections by major designers make fashionable label-conscious dressing possible for the middle class. Fashions are adapted for mass production by the major international garment industries including New York, Los Angeles, Paris, and Milan.

North American fashion is distinctive because of its casualness and is recognizably more informal than in Europe. North American informality in dress is a strong part of American and Canadian popular culture. North American designers often find inspiration in the imaginative attire worn by youths. For its fashion sources, North American style is dependent on what people on the streets are wearing and more often come from popular sources, such as urban centers, neighborhood streets, schools, sporting venues, music, TV, and movies.

For example, blue jeans are probably the single most representative article of North American clothing. During the 1950s, actors made blue jeans fashionable by wearing them in films, and jeans became part of the image of teenage angst and rebelliousness. This fashion statement exploded in the 1960s and 70s as blue jeans became a fundamental part of the youth culture focused on social reforms, civil rights, and antiwar protests. Musicians in particular adopted blue jean fashion as an expression of their counter-culture songs. By the late 70s, almost everyone in the North America wore blue jeans, and young people around the world sought them. As designers began to create more sophisticated styles of blue jeans and to adjust their fit, jeans began to express the North American emphasis on informality and the importance of subtlety of detail. By achieving the right look and highlighting the right label, blue jeans, despite their laborer origins, ironically embodied the status consciousness of North American fashion and the eagerness to adopt the latest trend.

The fashion industry in North America, along with its companion cosmetics industry, has become a major source of direct and collateral revenue for the general entertainment industry. Especially notable during the last few decades is the incorporation of sports logos and styles, from athletic shoes to tennis shirts and baseball caps, into standard international wardrobes. Informality is enshrined in the wardrobes created by world-famous North American designers whose names and trademarks have become an integral part of the entertainment industry. Successful clothing designers license their names, and put their distinctive marks on a wide range of diverse objects and accessories. Their custom design clothes are worn by entertainment celebrities and sold as merchandising. Their images grace the covers of pop culture magazines and fill the pages of the lucrative fashion magazine industry. Television shows are dedicated to fashion and the music industry uses cutting-edge fashion effectively in music videos. Product placement of garment lines and designer logos in TV programs, music videos, photographs, and films is a key marketing tool. Many famous artists and celebrities market their own personal clothing line. For example, the rap and hip-hop music industry has successfully converged with the fashion business to spawn multiple clothing and accessory lines, and enhance product merchandising.

Along with designers and super models, fashion photographers have become celebrities in their own right. Fashion photography illustrates and documents styles of dress and is used both as a sales tool in advertising and as a means of legitimizing and establishing new fashions as they emerge. The many talented photographers in the field produce a level of work that is often well above the commercial and is studied, ranked and collected as a form of social documentation and art.

The fashion business is rife with unauthorized copying but mostly free of infringement lawsuits like the ones the major record labels and film studios frequently file. Because of the rapidity of changing styles, copyright in designs is difficult to enforce. Copies or "knockoffs" are a reality of the industry. Some enterprises never create any original designs, instead specializing in knockoffs. The risk of confusion is the key legal test of whether a knockoff has crossed the line to forgery. A company can't copyright a design, but it can register elements of that design as trademarks. But for most of the fashion industry, copying is a way of life. It's expensive and risky to actually create new designs. It's cheaper and easier to simply knockoff successful ones. Typically, designers just let the copies go. After all, new designs will come out in a couple of months, and lawsuits are time-consuming, expensive and plaintiffs are never really sure whether or not they will win. Successful designers thus prefer to focus on the protection of their trademarks.

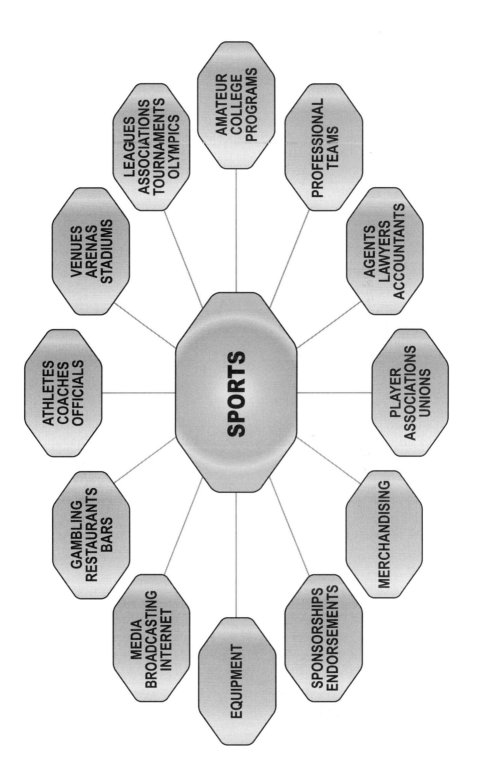

131

# 13.  SPORTS

The sports industry identifies and connects North Americans with mass entertainment culture. Billions of dollars are poured into sports and their related enterprises, affecting the economy, entertainment habits, leisure time, disposable income, and clothing styles. Sports have become one of the most visible expressions of popular culture, with millions of North Americans both personally participating and enjoying sports as spectators. Live sporting events converge with radio, television and Internet broadcasting, as well as merchandising. Music and performers are often featured at sports venues and during broadcasts. Motion pictures and video games feature sports stories and showcase sports heroes. Sports Hall of Fame museums are visited by millions of people year round.

Governing bodies, organizations, leagues, and associations regulate professional and amateur competition in several sports, ranging from the international Olympic Games down to local amateur leagues. While public subsidies and sponsorships support the immense network of outdoor and indoor amateur sports (sports in which competitors are not directly paid for their efforts), recreation, and athletic competitions, the majority of professional sports activities are privately funded. Most commercial basketball, baseball, football, hockey, and soccer teams reflect large private investments. Although the majority of sports teams are privately owned, they play in stadiums that are usually financed by taxpayer-provided subsidies. Taxpayer dollars also provide some financing for lucrative college sporting events. Tickets, parking, advertising, concessions, and merchandising sales form the bulk of a venue's revenue source, while broadcasting rights for television and radio are the key source of revenue for professional franchises and amateur sporting events.

Sports programming on television is an enormous business, and sports events are widely viewed among North Americans as cultural experiences. Sports broadcasting fills vast amount of television and radio programming time with several stations devoted entirely to sporting events and sports news. Professional wrestling, viewed by many as an organized theater sport, has utilized the power and reach of television to great benefit. North Americans watch sports on local, network, cable, and specialty satellite television. Many sports fans share televised moments of excitement and triumph throughout the year. Professional teams, from cities across North America, play a regular schedule that culminates in the championship series. The winner is awarded the league's top prize, for example: the National Football League (NFL) fall and early winter season culminates with the ultimate sports entertainment event – the Super Bowl; the National Hockey League (NHL) and National Basketball Association (NBA) championships are presented each spring; and, the Major League Baseball (MLB) spring and summer season gears towards its World Series in the early fall. The Olympic Games and World Cup Soccer, watched by millions of people worldwide every two and four years respectively, similarly rivet viewers to their televisions as they watch outstanding world-class athletes compete on behalf of their nations.

Commercial and mass media sports have permitted sports heroes to gain international prominence and become fixtures of the consumer culture. As well-known faces/bodies/personalities, sports celebrities, entrepreneurs, promoters, team owners, managers, coaches, cheerleaders, and even sportscasters are hired to endorse products and appear in films. Sports stars are internationally recognized figures, renowned not only as great athletes but as personalities that branch out into others areas of the entertainment industry. Famous sports figures are commonly regarded as extremely popular entertainers.

Although televised games remove the viewing public from direct contact with events, they do not diminished the fervor of team identification nor dampen the enthusiasm for athletic participation. With blanket coverage of sports events by newspapers, the Internet, radio and television, sports consumes a large percentage of people's free time. As North Americans enjoy more leisure time, and as the entertainment media and advertising emphasize muscular bodies, sports have become a significant component of many people's lives. North Americans take part in individual sports of all kinds and personally participate in more varied sporting activities and athletic clubs – increasing the demand for gear and driving sports equipment sales. Many North Americans now invest significant amounts of money in sports equipment, designer clothing, and gym memberships. As a result, more people are dressing in sporty styles of clothing. Sports logos and athletic fashions have become common aspects of the overall wardrobe of both men and women. A second continuing long-term fashion trend is the increasing importance of casual and sports attire. Sports have even influenced the consumer products people buy to reflect sporty lifestyles or to emulate their favorite sports heroes. The licensing of sports trademarks (team and individual names & logos) generates both revenue and brand recognition.

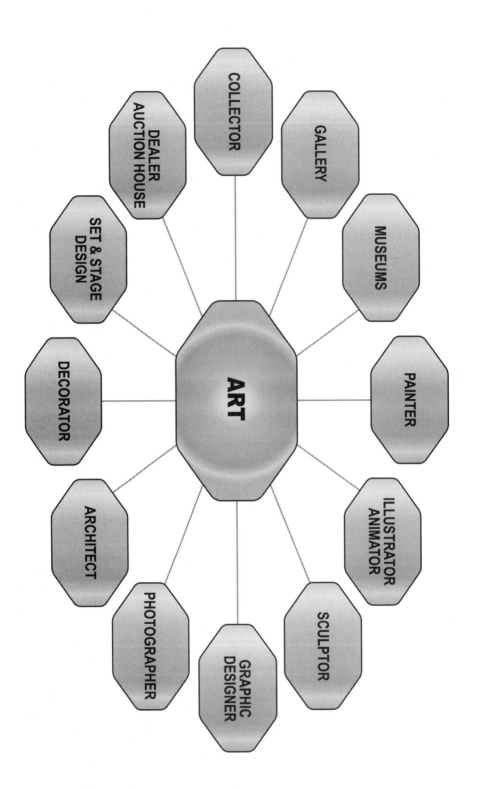

COLLECTOR

DEALER
AUCTION HOUSE

GALLERY

SET & STAGE
DESIGN

MUSEUMS

ART

DECORATOR

PAINTER

ARCHITECT

ILLUSTRATOR
ANIMATOR

PHOTOGRAPHER

SCULPTOR

GRAPHIC
DESIGNER

# 14. ART

Art is the use of skill and imagination in the creation of aesthetic objects, environments, or experiences that can be shared with the public. In other words, art is a disciplined activity that may be limited to skill or expanded to include a distinctive way of looking at the world. Art often combines practical and aesthetic functions, as is the case when utilized in the entertainment industry. The term art may also designate one of a number of modes of expression conventionally categorized by the medium utilized or the form of the product. The word "art" is derived from the Latin "ars," meaning "skill." Drawing, illustration, sculpture, graphics, decorations, paintings, filmmaking, music, dance, literature, and many other types of aesthetic expression are viewed as art and all of them collectively as the arts.

Art is skill at performing a set of specialized actions. Art in its broader meaning, however, involves both skill and creative imagination in a musical, literary, visual, or performance context. Art provides those who produce it and the people that observe it with an experience that might be emotional, intellectual, aesthetic, or a combination of these qualities. A distinction arises between "artist" and "artisan," the latter being a skilled manual worker who gives considerable attention to the utilitarian, the former denoting capacity for imaginative invention often attaining purely aesthetic purposes. Although "the arts" may be taken as comprising the verbal and musical as well as the visual, art is usually assumed to mean the visual arts, painting, sculpture, drawing, decorative arts, photography, printmaking, and architecture.

Traditionally, the arts are divided into the "fine" and the "liberal" arts. The latter are concerned with mental skills of expression in language, speech, rhetoric, and reasoning. The fine arts, a translation of the French "beaux-arts," are more concerned primarily with purely aesthetic or "beautiful" ends created by the artist's physical skills. Many forms of expression combine aesthetic concerns with utilitarian purposes, such as architecture, fashion, and advertising design. The decorative or applied arts, such as pottery, metalwork, furniture, tapestry, and enamel, are often useful arts and considered "crafts". The various arts thus occupy different regions along a spectrum that ranges from purely utilitarian purposes at one end to purely aesthetic purposes at the other. This should by no means be taken as a rigid scheme, however. Even within one form of art, motives may vary widely, making it difficult to distinguish between art that is purely aesthetic and art that is also practical. Thus a woodworker may create a highly functional work (a cabinet, for example) that is at the same time beautiful, or he/she may create works that have no purpose whatever beyond being admired. Another traditional system of classification, applied to the fine arts, establishes such categories as writing or literature (including drama, poetry, novels, music lyrics, and scripts), the visual arts (painting, sculpture, set/stage/costume design), the graphic arts (painting, illustration, design, and other forms expressed on flat surfaces), the plastic arts (modeling, sculpture), the decorative arts (furniture design, mosaic, masks, enamelwork), the performing arts (theater, films, television, music, dance), and architecture (including interior design).

As mentioned, art requires technical skill. The artist tries to create order out of the seemingly diverse and random experiences of the world and attempts to understand and appreciate the world and to convey personal experiences to others. The artist selects qualitative perceptions and arranges them to express cultural and personal understanding. Despite changes in the artist's view or the public taste, a work of art has permanent validity as an aesthetic statement at a particular place and time. Although artists may be uniquely impelled by their own creative energies, they are also very much products of their culture, communities and societies.

An artist's medium affects the style of the work. Thus, an illustrator must treat paper differently from a computer screen; a musician achieves different effects with guitars than with trumpets; a writer must meet certain demands of movie scripts that might be irrelevant to the novel. In addition, the subject of art is largely dictated by the society that supports it. Art is made for many reasons: for commemoration of people and events, for religious devotion, for adornment of utilitarian objects, for personal expression, and for entertainment. It is also created on many scales including tall buildings, massive cathedrals, huge motion picture sets, and elaborate theater backdrops and decors.

Art in all its categories is considered an essential part of human achievement, and some of its many, varied creators are ranked among the most famous and celebrated people of the world. Much leisure time is spent viewing their works in museums and art galleries; however, mass media provides much larger audiences. The business of art thus goes beyond traditional art dealers. The entertainment industry employs legions of artists for their works and services in a variety of categories including set/stage/costume/prop designs, marketing and merchandising, as well as, animation drawing and graphics. Generally speaking, works of art are "entertaining" and thus form an important category that intertwines with all the other areas of the entertainment industry.

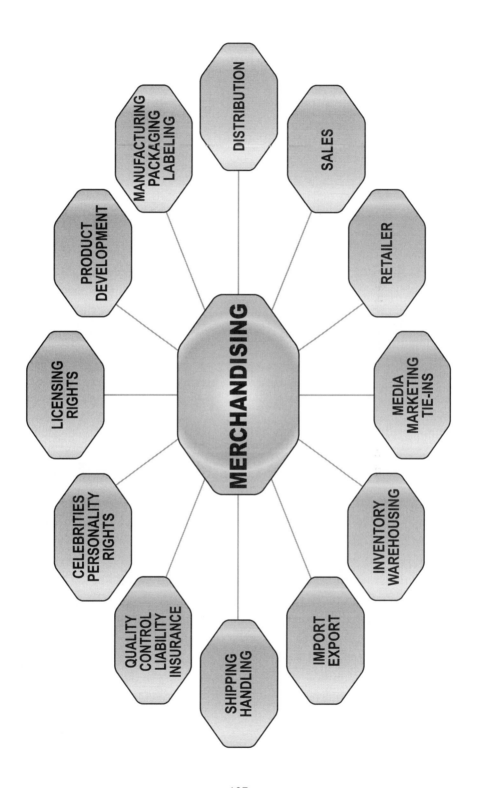

MERCHANDISING

DISTRIBUTION

MANUFACTURING PACKAGING LABELING

SALES

PRODUCT DEVELOPMENT

RETAILER

LICENSING RIGHTS

MEDIA MARKETING TIE-INS

CELEBRITIES PERSONALITY RIGHTS

INVENTORY WAREHOUSING

QUALITY CONTROL LIABILITY INSURANCE

SHIPPING HANDLING

IMPORT EXPORT

# 15.  MERCHANDISING


Merchandising is the manufacturing, wholesaling, distributing, marketing, and selling or retailing of products to the public. Product merchandising is a major part of the entertainment business. Entertainment merchandising includes products related to an artist or entertainer's business, works, copyrighted materials, trademark rights, and personality (name, likeness, character, reputation). Endorsements are the direct association by the entertainer with previously or specially manufactured products or services, or a cause or institution that implies approval by the artist of such endorsement. A commercial tie-in or tie-up is the use of a celebrity's artist personality rights in the context of an advertisement. Merchandisers frequently support entertainment events and artists through sponsorships. Sponsorships are the exchange of products, services or money for advertisements and public exposure.

Merchandisers oversee the marketing, planning and control of goods or services while providing effective product development, and ensuring the proper commodity is available at a time, place, price, and quantity conducive to profitable sale. For the manufacturer, merchandising involves product planning and management. For the retailer or wholesaler it includes selecting colors, sizes, and styles preferred by the customers or trade. Strategic placement and correct timing of a product are particularly important for fashion goods, for seasonal merchandise, and for fads with a rate of sale that fluctuates significantly. The price is usually determined so as to sell merchandise quickly and at a profit satisfactory to the merchandiser. The quantity ordered should create a supply large enough to satisfy all potential customers but should not be excessive to a point that might necessitate price reductions in order to bring about sufficient sales.

An early example of successful entertainment merchandising involved the legendary 1960s rock band, The Beatles. Beatlemania was the term employed to describe the excitement generated by the musical group. Guided by their dedicated manager, Beatlemania changed international pop culture. It affected North American society in numerous ways, including hairstyle, fashion and merchandising. Since then, many other entertainers and their works have benefited from lucrative merchandising deals. The most important recent development in popular music has been the rise of rap, which originated as a genre of folk music growing out of black youth street culture in the South Bronx community of New York City in the mid-1970s. Although the term rap is often used interchangeably with hip-hop, the latter term encompasses the street subculture that rap music is simply one part of. The term "hip-hop" derives from one of the earliest phrases used in rap. In addition to rap music, the hip-hop subculture also comprises other forms of expression, including graffiti art and break dancing as well as a unique fashion sense and jargon vocabulary. Over the past two decades, rap music has developed and influenced music merchandising to the point that certain rap artists generate more revenue from product sales and endorsements than from their music recordings.

Entertainment merchandising benefits all categories of the industry and in many cases provides additional revenues to an enterprise's main activities. Ancillary enterprises are often involved in the exploitation of merchandising rights owned by a parent company.

## MERCHANDISING RIGHTS

## PERSONALITY – COPYRIGHT – TRADEMARK

## MERCHANDISING DEAL POINTS

**LICENSING OF RIGHTS – TERM & TERRITORY**
**COPYRIGHT & TRADEMARK GUARANTEES**
**EXCLUSIVITY – PRODUCT DEVELOPMENT**
**ITEMS LIST – PRODUCT QUALITY CONTROL**
**APPROVAL OF ITEMS – CREATIVE CONTROL**
**LABELING & PACKAGING – MANUFACTURING**
**INVENTORY – SHIPPING – WAREHOUSING**
**MARKETING/PROMOTIONS/ADVERTISING**
**SALES NETWORK & DISTRIBUTION**
**PRODUCT LIABILITY INSURANCE**
**COMPENSATION/FEE/ROYALTY/ADVANCE/BONUS**
**PAYMENT SCHEDULE/ACCOUNTING/INSPECTION**
**SELL-OFF RIGHTS – OPTING OUT – MORALITY**

# 16.  JOBS & CAREERS

The various branches of the Entertainment industry provide jobs and careers for thousands of people around the world, many of them educated in specialized schools or trained on the job. Workers can find full and part-time employment or offer their services as freelance laborers. Various unions, associations, societies, and guilds representing workers, guarantee minimum working and pay conditions. Volunteering and internships (low paying or unpaid) often lead to good paying jobs.

The entertainment industry workforce
is divided into 3 general categories:

**Making Entertainment**
(creation/production)

**Selling Entertainment**
(sales/marketing)

**Business of Entertainment**
(management/business/administration/legal)

The following list constitutes a diverse sampling (in no particular order) of entertainment-related jobs and careers.

writer – artist – actor – musician – singer – composer – film director – lyrists – journalist – critic – playwright – publisher – editor – librarian – talent coordinator – transcriber – budget planner – talent agent – concert booking agent – arts and culture administrator – union officer – audience researcher – career advisor – entertainment lawyer – broadcasting executive – business manager – theatre manager – concert promoter – product manager – educational director – market research director – entertainment director – nightclub manager – orchestra manager – personal manager – professional manager – player agent – program director

– talent director – music director – programming consultant – project director – record company executive – recording studio manager – stage manager – road manager – art studio manager – business attorney – talent agency manager – model agency manager – media coordinator – tour manager – advertising account executive – consumer researcher – festival organizer – radio tracker – podcaster – creative director – disc jockey – jingle writer – singing coach – program supervisor – promotional manager – ratings agent – athlete – coach – referee – competition judge – talent scout – general manager – sportscaster – broadcasting station broker – multimedia coordinator – music merchant – salesperson – product rights manager – product wholesaler – product distributor – publicist – personal security agent – ticket sales agent – music arranger – audio technician – conductor – recording engineer – choreographer – dancer – stage designer – fashion consultant – make-up artist – hair stylist – stage supervisor – lighting designer – instrumentalist – stunt coordinator – floor manager – festival programmer – pyrotechnic coordinator – personal appearances booking agent – scenic designer – executive producer – computer music programmer – digital audio/video engineer – Foley artist – equipment designer – equipment maintenance technician – instrument manufacturer – audio professional – mastering technician – piano tuner – website designer – copyright researcher – trademark agent – intellectual property attorney – paralegal – accountant – fiscal planner – grants/loans advisor – customs agent – immigration/customs lawyer – educator – media consultant – e-commerce consultant – sales representative – illustrator – circus performer – acting coach – transportation/travel coordinator – musicologist – translator – copyist – reporter – press consultant – event planner – sound/video editor – casting agent – personal assistant – historian – interviewer – conservationist – librettist – theater dresser – museum director/ curator/preservation – master of ceremonies – voice-overs – animator – festival talent coordinator – event security agent – gaffer – day player – craft services – executive producer – art director – producer – director – writer – cinematographer – film editor – associate producer – stunt performer – storyboard coordinator – production manager – unit production manager – line producer – continuity person – camera operator – assistant camera operator – film loader – stead cam operator – production sound mixer –

boom operator – key grip – dolly grip – best boy – ADR editor – music mixer – FX coordinator – post-production supervisor – matte artist – location manager – property master – leadman – set designer – set dresser – costume designer – costumer – make-up artist – body make-up artist – hairdresser – dialogue coach – production office coordinator – production assistant – unit publicist – production caterer – craft services – negative cutter –story editor – press agent – budget manager/administrator – set carpenter – program buyer – driver – etiquette coach – historical consultant/researcher – housing coordinator – film stage medic – computer programmer – talk show hosts – newscaster – sports announcer – weathercaster – director of photography – imaging digital technician – special effects operator – tax planner – talent finder – intern – radio host – radio advertising sales rep – board operator – general sales manager – playwright – dramaturge – voice & dialect coach – fight director – visual effects producer/designer/director – stagehands – copywriter – songwriter – back-up singer – A&R (artist and repertoire) – project coordinator – rack jobber – international sales agent – record marketing – promotions rep – public relations – press – radio tracking – record producer – film/TV studio manager – sound engineer – studio mixer – sound stage designer – video producer – video director – choreographer – dancer – actor – cameraperson – clothes/make-up/hair stylist – event booking agent – foreign sales representative – tour coordinator (hotels/transportation/food etc.) – crew & roadies – sound & light technician – pyrotechnics – catering – equipment/artist transportation – music festival and radio programmer – photographer – webmaster – business affairs – nightclub/radio DJ (disc jockey) – video programmer – VJ (video jockey) – advertising – TV/film licensing manager – merchandising – fan club organizer – personal trainer – software programmer – new media & technology consultant – broadcaster – royalty – TV director – collection agent – unions/guilds/industry associations representative – art dealer – guitar technician – mascot performer – theme park designer – fashion designer – event manager – graphic artist/designer – marketing representative – advertising buyer – foreign rights buyer – announcer – proof reader – indexer – technical advisor – syndication buyer – animal trainer – musical director – reviewer – sports statistician – head hunter – cataloguer – webcaster

# EPILOGUE

Entertainment fills the leisure and recreational time of most North Americans. As an industry it is dynamic and constantly changing. For the purposes of this treatise, I chose to broadly define the term "entertainment" as "people entertained by the works or performances of others." Upon completion of this captivating and stimulating entertainment voyage, I must restate that this book was only a general overview of the topic. Many more volumes are needed to do justice to the popular entertainment categories presented herein; and additional ones could certainly have been added. For example, recreational travel is not dealt with in this tome, however, one could argue that personal freestyle travel, organized group travel, and cruise travel are particular forms of entertainment. The same could also be said about amusement/theme parks, resorts & casinos, and, entertainment theme bars & restaurants. Some forms of entertainment lead to the indirect popularity of ancillary forms of recreation. For example, organized athletics spawned and continues to drive the lucrative, legalized sports gambling sector.

A growing trend in the field of entertainment is the "self-production" phenomenon. Technology is making it easier and a great deal cheaper for all kinds of entertainers to create, self-produce, and sell their own wares. For instance, the self-publishing of books has allowed thousands of authors to write, publish, and sell their manuscripts. Also, more and more musicians record, self-produce, market, and sell their own music.

This book purposely dealt with the convergence as well as the consolidation of the entertainment industry. Consolidation is "the act of combining into an integral whole". In the end, one can argue that modern show biz is the consolidation of business and art.

As for the future of the entertainment industry ?

Well, let's all sit back, watch, listen, and enjoy the show

... or better yet, join the parade!

Thanks for the read,
Mark Vinet

Academy of Canadian Cinema and Television (ACCT), Toronto, Canada.

Academy of Motion Picture Arts and Sciences (AMPAS), Los Angeles, California, USA.

Access Copyright, The Canadian Copyright Licensing Agency. Toronto, Ontario, Canada.

Agins, T., *The End of Fashion: The Mass Marketing of the Clothing Business*. Perennial Currents, 2000.

Aitken, Hugh G., *Syntony and Spark: The Origins of Radio*. Princeton University Press, 1985.

Alliance of Artists and Recording Companies (AARC), Alexandria, Virginia, USA.

Alliance of Canadian Cinema, Television and Radio Artists (ACTRA), Toronto, Canada.

Alliance of Motion Picture and Television Producers (AMPTP), Encino, California, USA.

American Actors' Equity Association (AEA), Los Angeles, USA.

American Bar Association (Intellectual Property Law section), *Forum on the Entertainment & Sports Industries: Current Legal & Business Issues in the Motion Picture & Television Industry (Production & Distribution)*, Chicago, Illinois, 1993, 2005.

American Federation of Television and Radio Artists (AFTRA), New York, USA.

American Society of Composers, Authors and Publishers (ASCAP), New York, NY, USA.

Anderssen, Anton. *Anton's Publishing Primer: How to Publish Your First Book*. Hartforth Publishing, 2002.

Archives Nationales du Québec. Montreal, Quebec, Canada.

Archives of Ontario. Toronto, Ontario, Canada.

Arnheim, Rudolf, *Radio (History of Broadcasting: Radio to Television)*, Arno Press reprint edition 1971.

Arnold, Denis. *The New Oxford Companion to Music*, 2 vol. Oxford University Press, 1983, reprint 1990.

Art Dealers Association of America (ADAA), New York, USA.

Art Dealers Association of Canada (ADAC), Toronto, Canada.

Ashelford, Jane, *The Art of Dress: Clothes and Society, 1500-1914,* Antique Collectors' Club, 1996.

Association of American Publishers (AAP), New York, NY, USA.

Association of Canadian Archivists (ACA), Ottawa, Ontario, Canada.

Association of Canadian Publishers (ACP), Toronto, Canada.

Association of English-language Publishers of Quebec (AELAQ), Montreal, Canada.

Association of Professional Sports Agents (APSA), UK (England, Scotland, Wales).

Audio Cine Films Inc. Montreal, Quebec, Canada.

Audio-Video Licensing Agency Inc. (AVLA), Toronto, Canada.

Avalon, Moses. *Confessions of a Record Producer: How to Survive the Scams & Shams of the Music Business,* Backbeat Books, 2nd edition, 2002.

Bach, Steven, *Final Cut: Art, Money, and Ego in the Making of Heaven's Gate, the Film That Sank United Artists*, Newmarket Press; Revised edition, 1999.

Baines, Anthony. *The Oxford Companion to Musical Instruments*. Oxford University Press, 1992.

Baker, B. *Guerrilla Music Marketing Handbook: 201 Self-Promotion Ideas for Songwriters, Musicians & Bands*, Spotlight Pub., 2001.

Baker, Theodore. *Baker's Biographical Dictionary of Musicians*, 8th ed., rev. Nicolas Slonimsky, 1992.

Baker, William J., *Sports in the Western World,* Rowman & Littlefield Pub, 1983.

Balliett, Whitney. *American Musicians II: Seventy-two Portraits in Jazz*. 2nd ed. Oxford Univ. Pr., 1996.

Barnouw, Erik. *Tube of Plenty: The Evolution of American Television*, Oxford University Press 1992.

Barranger, Milly S., *Theatre: A Way of Seeing, Understanding Plays,* and *Theatre: Past and Present.* Wadsworth Publishing; 5th edition 2001.

Barzun, Jacques. Simple and Direct: *A Rhetoric for Writers,* University Of Chicago Press; Rev. ed., 1994.

Baskerville, David. *The Music Business Handbook & Career Guide, 6th & 7th eds.* Sage Pub. 1995, 2001.

Batten, Joseph. *Joe Batten's Book: The Story of Sound Recording,* Rockliff, 1956.

Batterberry, Michael, *Fashion: The Mirror of History,* Cresent, revised edition, 1987.

Batterby, Michael and Ariane, *Mirror, Mirror: A Social History of Fashion*, Holt Rinehart & Winston, 1979.

Belleville, Nyree. *Booking, Promoting and Marketing Your Music: A Complete Guide for Bands and Solo Artists*, Hal Leonard, Artistpro, 2000.

Benagh, Jim. *ABC's wide world of sports encyclopedia*. Stadia Sports Pub. Rev. ed. 1974; *Monday Morning Quarterback*, Henry Holt & Co. 1st ed., 1983; *Incredible athletic feats,* Bantam Pathfind, 1972.

Berklee College of Music. Boston, Massachusetts, USA.

*Berne Convention For The Protection Of Literary And Artistic Works*, WIPO.

Bessler, Ian. *2004 Songwriter's Market: 1700 + Places to Market Your Songs*, Writers Digest Books, 2003.

Bibliothèque de l'Université de Montréal. Montreal, Quebec, Canada.

Bibliothèque nationale de France. Paris, France.

Bibliothèque Nationale du Québec (BNQ), Grande Bibliothèque, Montreal, Canada.

*Billboard 100th Anniversary Issue: 1894-1994* & *Billboard International Buyer's Guide*, BPI Com. 1994.

Bindas, Kenneth J., ed. *America's Musical Pulse: Popular Music in 20th Century Society*. Praeger, 1992.

Black, J.A., Garland, M., Kennett, F. *A History of Fashion*, William Morrow, 1985.

Blume, J. *6 Steps to Songwriting Success: Comprehensive Guide to Writing & Marketing Hit Songs,* Billboard, 2004.

Bogdanov, V. ed. et al. *All Music Guide to Rock: Definitive Guide to Rock, Pop, Soul, R&B, & Rap* and *All Music Guide to Hip-Hop: Definitive Guide to Rap & Hip-Hop*. Backbeat Bks, 2003.

Boucher, François, *20,000 Years of Fashion,* Harry N. Abrams, 1967. repr. 1987.

Bourdieu, Pierre. *On Television*, The New Press, 2001.

Braheny, John. *The Craft and Business of Songwriting,* Writer's Digest Books, 2nd edition, 2001.

British Archives & British Museum. London, United Kingdom.

Broadcast Music Inc. (BMI), New York, USA.

Brooks, T, *Complete Directory to Prime Time Network TV Shows, 1946-Present*, Ballantine, 8th ed. 2003.

Brown, Gene. *Movie Time: A Chronology of Hollywood and the Movie Industry from its Beginnings to the Present*, MacMillan, 1995.

Brunet, Alain. *Le disque ne tourne pas rond*, Éditions Coronet, 2003.

Brunson-Sarrabo, Yolanda. The Ins & Outs of the Fashion Industry-From a Fashion Insider, iUniverse, 2005.

Burns, Leslie Davis & Bryant, Nancy O. *The Business of Fashion*, Fairchild Books & Visuals, 2nd ed, 2001.

Busby, L. J., and Parker, D. L., *The Art and Science of Radio,* Prentice Hall College, 1984.

Cable & Telecommunications Association for Marketing (CTAM), Alexandria, Virginia, USA.

California Film Commission (CFC), Hollywood, California, USA.

Campbell, R.A., *Media and Culture: An Introduction to Mass Communication,* Bedford/St.Martin's, 2003.

Canada Council for the Arts (CCA), Ottawa, Canada.

Canadian Academy of Recording Arts and Sciences, Juno awards (CARAS), Toronto, Canada.

Canadian Actors' Equity Association (CAEA), Toronto, Canada.

Canadian Artists' Representation Copyright Collective (CARCC), Ottawa, Canada.

Canadian Association of Internet Providers (CAIP), Ottawa, Canada.

Canadian Association of Music Libraries, Archives & Documentation Centres. York University, Toronto.

Canadian Audio-Visual Certification Office (CAVCO); Canadian or Video Production Tax Credit (CPTC); Book Industry Development Program, Canada Magazine Fund (CMF), Depart. Cdn Heritage, Ottawa.

Canadian Authors Association (CAA), Toronto, Canada.

Canadian Broadcasters Rights Agency (CBRA), Ottawa, Canada.

Canadian Coalition for Fair Digital Access (CCFDA), Ottawa, Ontario, Canada.

Canadian Conference of the Arts (CCA), Directory of the Arts, Ottawa, Canada.

Canadian Country Music Association (CCMA). Woodbridge, Ontario, Canada.

Canadian Electroacoustic Community (CEC), Concordia University, Montreal, Canada.

Canadian and Television Production Association (CFTPA) & Producers Audiovisual Collective of Canada (PACC), Toronto, Canada.

Canadian Independent Record Production Association (CIRPA), Toronto, Canada.

Canadian Intellectual Property Office (CIPO), Industry Canada, Hull, Quebec, Canada; Canada Copyright Act, Consolidated Statutes and Regulations, Copyright Act (R.S. 1985, c. C-42); Canada Trademarks Act, Consolidated Statutes and Regulations; Canada Industrial Design Act, Consolidated Statutes and Regulations; Canada Integrated Circuit Topography Act, Consolidated Statutes and Regulations; Canada Patent Act, Consolidated Statutes and Regulations.

Canadian Internet Registration Authority (CIRA), Ottawa, Ontario, Canada.

Canadian League of Composers (CLC), Toronto, Canada.

Canadian Library Association (CLA); Canadian Association of College & University Libraries (CACUL); Canadian Association of Public Libraries (CAPL), Ottawa, Canada

Canadian Music Centre (CMC), Toronto, Canada.

Canadian Music Publishers Association (CMPA), Toronto, Canada.

Canadian Music Week Music & Entertainment Conference (CMW), Toronto, Canada.

Canadian Musical Reproduction Rights Agency Limited (CMRRA) Toronto, Canada.

Canadian Private Copying Collective (CPCC), Toronto, Canada.

Canadian Radio-television and Telecommunications Commission (CRTC), Ottawa, Canada.

Canadian Recording Industry Association (CRIA), Toronto, Canada.

Canadian Retransmission Collective (CRC), Toronto, Ontario, Canada.

Canadian Video Services (CVS), Mississauga, Ontario, Canada.

Caputo, Tony C. *Simple & Direct: How to Self-Publish Your Own Comic Book: The Complete Resource Guide to the Business, Production, Distribution, Marketing and Promotion of Comic Books,* Watson-Guptill Publications, 1997.

145

Carter, Sebastian. *Twentieth-Century Type Designers*, W. W. Norton & Company, 1995.

Center for Popular Music, Middle Tennessee State University, USA.

Charmasson, Henri. *Patents, Copyrights & Trademarks for Dummies*, For Dummies, 2004.

Ciaravino, Helene. *How to Publish Your Poetry: A Complete Guide to Finding the Right Publishers for Your Work,* Square One Publishers, 2001.

Citron, Stephen. *Songwriting: A Complete Guide to the Craft,* Limelight Editions, reprint, 2004.

Clancy, Deirdre, *Costume since 1945: Couture, Street Style, and Anti-Fashion,* Drama Publishers, 1996.

Clarke, Donald. *The Penguin Encyclopedia of Popular Music.* Viking, 1989.

Cole, David. *Complete Guide to Book Marketing,* Allworth Press, 1999.

Coleridge, Nicholas, *The Fashion Conspiracy.* Harpercollins, 1988.

Comer, D., *The Internet Book*: *Everything You Need to Know About Computer Networking and How the Internet Works.* 3rd edition, 2000.

*Copyright and the Music Industry*, International Association of Entertainment Lawyers (IAEL), 2005.

Copyright Clearance Center, Inc. (CCC), Danvers, Massachusetts, USA.

*Copyright Law of the United States of America and Related Laws.* Superintendent of Documents, Washington DC, 2005.

*Counseling Clients in the Entertainment Industry: , Theater, Music Publishing; Sound Recordings, The Computer & Video Game Industry, Sports, The Computer & Video Game Industry; Content and Entertainment License Agreements,* Practicing Law Institute, 2005; *Hot Topics in Entertainment Law: Recent Court Decisions; Advanced Licensing Agreements 2005.*

Crawford, T. *Starting Your Career As a Freelance Photographer*, Allworth Press, 2003; *The Artist-Gallery Partnership: A Practical Guide to Consigning Art,* Watson-Guptill Publications, 2nd edition, 1998.

Crumlish, Christian, *The ABCs of the Internet*, Sybex Inc ., 2nd edition, 1997.

Curran, Mark, W. *Sell Your Music: How To Profitably Sell Your Own Recordings Online.* NMD Bks, 2001.

Daniel, Ralph Thomas, contributor, *The Harvard Brief Dictionary of Music.* Fine Comms. repr. ed. 1997.

Daria, Irene, *The Fashion Cycle,* Simon & Schuster, 1990.

Davis, Richard. Complete Guide to Scoring, Berklee Press Publications, 2000.

DeCurtis, Anthony, eds. *Rolling Stone Illustrated History of Rock & Roll*. 3rd ed. Random House, 1992.

Dennis, E. E., and Pease, E., eds., *Radio as the Forgotten Medium,* Transaction Publishers, 1994.

Dern, D.P. *Internet Business Handbook: The Insider's Internet Guide*, 1999.

Devlin, Polly, *The Vogue Book of Fashion Photography,* McNally & Loftin Publishers, 1984.

Directors Guild of America (DGA), Los Angeles, California, USA.

Directors Guild of Canada (DGC), Toronto, Canada.

Directors Rights Collective of Canada (DRCC), Toronto, Ontario, Canada.

*Directory of the Arts 2005*, Canadian Conference of the Arts, Ottawa, Canada.

Dombrower, Eddie, *The Art of Interactive Entertainment Design*, Computing Mcgraw-Hill 1998.

Drabinsky, Garth. *Motion pictures & the arts in Canada: Business & the law.* McGraw-Hill Ryerson, 1976.

Editors Association of Canada (EAC), Toronto, Canada.

Educational Rights Collective of Canada (ERCC), Toronto, Canada.

*Educator's Guide to the Internet*, Virginia Space Grant Consortium Staff, 1997.

*Encyclopedia of Music in Canada*, Introductions to EMC: second edition, electronic version, May 2001.

Ewing, Elizabeth, *History of Twentieth-Century Fashion* Rowman & Littlefield Publishers, 1992.

Ewing, William, *The Idealizing Vision: The Art of Fashion Photography,* Aperture, 1991.

Falkner, L.J. *The Magic of Writing: How to Write and Publish the Book that is Inside You,* iUniverse, 2003.

Farber, Donald C. (general editor), *Entertainment Industry Contracts*, Matthew Bender & Co., 2005.

Farber, Robert, *The Fashion Photographer,* Watson-Guptill Publications, 1981. repr. 1984.

Fashion Merchandising Association (FMA), Pittsburg State University, Pennsylvania, USA.

Field, Shelly. *Career Opportunities in the Music Industry*, Checkmark Books, 5th edition, 2004.

Finler, Joel, *The Hollywood Story*, Wallflower Press, 2003.

Fisher, Jeffrey P. *How to Make Money: Scoring Soundtracks and Jingles*, Artistpro, 1997.

Foreign Publishers Advertising Services Act, (1999, c. 23), Consolidated Statutes and Regulations of Canada.

Foundation to Assist Canadian Talent (VIDEOFACT), MuchMusic, CHUM Limited, Toronto, Canada.

Foundation to Assist Canadian Talent on Records (FACTOR), Toronto, Canada.

*Free Advice*, Cader Books, Cader Company Inc., 2002.

Frey, J.N. *How to Write a Damn Good Novel: A Step-by-Step No Nonsense Guide to Dramatic Storytelling*

Frings, V. S., *Fashion: From Concept to Consumer,* Prentice Hall, 8 edition, 2004.

Gammond, Peter. *The Oxford Companion to Popular Music.* Oxford, 1991.

*Geneva Convention for the Protection of Producers of Phonograms Against Unauthorized Duplication of Their Phonograms* of October 29, 1971. WIPO, Geneva, Switzerland.

Gershenfeld, A, and Loparco, M, and Barajas, C. *Game Plan: The Insider's Guide to Breaking In and Succeeding in the Computer and Video Game Business*, St. Martin's Griffin, 2003.

Golbin, Pamela. *Fashion Designers*, Watson-Guptill Publications, 2001.

Goldman, William, *Adventures in the Screen Trade*, Warner Books, 1989.

Goldstein, Jeri. *How To Be Your Own Booking Agent and Save Thousands Of Dollars: A Performing Artist's Guide To A Successful Touring Career*. New Music Times, 2000.

Gonzalez, J.S., *The 21st Century Intranet*, Prentice Hall, 1998.

Grauer, R., and Marx, G., *Essentials of the Internet*, Prentice Hall, 2d ed., 1997.

Green, D. C., *Radio Systems Technology,* Longman Scientific and Technical, 1990.

Greenberg, Martin J. *Sports law Practice*. Lexis Law Pub 2nd ed. 1998; with Hofmann, Dale, *Sport$Biz: An Irreverent Look at Big Business in Pro Sports*. Leisure Press, 1989.

Grossman, Wendy M.., *net.wars*, New York University Press, 1997.

Guild of Canadian Composers (GCC), Toronto, Canada.

Hafner, K. & Lyon, M., *Where Wizards Stay Up Late: The Origins Of The Internet.* Simon&Schuster, 1998.

Hall, Charles W. *Marketing in the Music Industry*. Prentice Hall, 2000.

Han, Holly. *Vault Career Guide to the Fashion Industry*, Vault, Inc., 2003.

Harris, Lesley Ellen. *Canadian copyright law: The indispensable guide for publishers, web professionals, writers, artists, filmmakers, teachers, librarians, archivists, curators, lawyers, and business people*. McGraw-Hill Ryerson, 3rd ed, 2001.

Harvard University, *American Judicial System*, Professor David R. Manwaring, 1992; Harvard University Libraries and Museums, Cambridge, Massachusetts, USA.

Hatschek, Keith. *How to Get a Job in the Music and Recording Industry*, Berklee Press Publications, 2001.

Hayes, Michael, and Dinsey, Stuart, *Games War: Video Games, A Business Review*, Bowerdean Pub, 1996.

Heil, Scott and T.W. Peck, eds. *Encyclopedia of American Industry, 2nd ed*. Detroit: Gale Research, 1998.

Herman, Deborah L. & Jeff, *Write the Perfect Book Proposal: 10 That Sold and Why*, Wiley; 2nd ed, 2001.

Herz, J. C., *Joystick Nation: How Videogames Ate Our Quarters, Won Our Hearts, and Rewired Our Minds*, Little Brown & Co, 1997.

Hitchcock, H.W., Sadie S., eds. *New Grove Dictionary of American Music*. Grove's Dictionaries, 1986.

Holt, Robert L. *How To Publish, Promote, & Sell Your Own Book* St. Martin's Griffin, 1986.

Holt, W. H., and Morgan, R. J., *The Web Dictionary,* Resolution Business, 1998.

Hughes, D. R., and Hendricks, D., "Spread-Spectrum Radio," *Scientific American*, April 1998.

Hughes, L. E. *Internet E-Mail: Protocols, Standards, and Implementation*, Artech House Publishers, 1998.

Hustwit, Gary. *Releasing an Independent Record*. Samuel French Trade, 1995.

Independent & Television Alliance (AFTA), Los Angeles, California, USA.

Intellectual Property Institute of Canada, Ottawa, Ontario, Canada

International Association for the Study of Popular Music (IASPM), Carleton University, Ottawa, Canada.

International Association of Music Libraries, Archives and Documentation Centres (IAML), Library and Archives Canada, Ottawa, Canada & Indiana University Bloomington, Indiana, USA.

International Confederation of Societies of Authors and Composers (CISAC), International ISWC (International Standard Musical Work Code) Agency, Neuilly sur Seine, France.

*International Convention For the Protection of Performers, Producers of Phonograms and Broadcasting Organizations* of 1961 (Rome Convention).

International Federation of Actors (FIA), London, UK.

International Federation of Reproduction Rights Organizations (IFRRO), Brussels, Belgium.

International Federation of the Phonographic Industry (IFPI), London, United Kingdom.

International Game Journalists Association (IGJA).

International Literary and Artistic Association, Paris, France; ALAI Canada, Montreal, Canada.

International Music Market (MIDEM), NRJ Music Awards, Cannes, France.

International Olympic Committee (IOC), Lausanne, Switzerland.

International Organization for Standardisation (ISO), Geneva, Switzerland.

International Recording Media Association (IRMA), Princeton, New Jersey, USA.

International Songwriters Association (ISA), London, UK.

Isenberg, Jerry, *Television Production*, 2000.

John Abbott College, Music Program. Ste. Anne de Bellevue, Quebec, Canada.

Katz, Ephraim, *The Film Encyclopedia*, HarperResource, 4th revised edition, 2001.

Kawa-Jump, S. *How to Publish Your Articles: A Complete Guide to Making the Right Publication Say Yes*, Square One Publishers, 2001.

Kawin, Bruce, *How Movies Work*, University of California Press, 1992,

Kehoe, B.P. *Zen and the Art of the Internet: A Beginner's Guide*, Prentice Hall, 4th ed. 1995.

Kent, Nicolas, *Naked Hollywood: Money and power in the movies today*. St. Martin's Press 1991.

Kottak, C.P., *Prime-Time Society: An Anthropological Analysis of Television & Culture*, Wadsworth, 1990.

Kraynak, Joe, *The Big Basics Book of the Internet*, Que Pub, 1996.

147

Kremer, John. *1001 Ways to Market Your Books,* Open Horizons, 5th edition, 2000.

Ladouceur, Yves. *Les affaires de la musique*, Tome 1/2/3. les Productions 12ᵉ Art Académie, 1996.

Larsen, Michael. *How to Write a Book Proposal*, Writer's Digest Books, 3rd edition, 2004.

Lathrop, Tad & Pettigrew, Jim. *This Business of Music Marketing and Promotion*, Billboard Bks, 2003.

Laver, James, *Costume and Fashion: A Concise History*, Thames & Hudson, 4th ed., 2002.

Law Society of Upper Canada, *Entertainment, Advertising & Media Law*. 1993, 2005.

Leonard, David P. *"The Canadian Music Industry", The Music Business Handbook & Career Guide, 4ᵗʰ & 5ᵗʰ editions* by David Baskerville. Sage Publications.

Lipovetsky, G. *Empire of Fashion: Dressing Modern Democracy*, trans. Porter, C. Princeton Univ. Pr, 2002.

Literary Translators Association Canada (LTAC), Concordia University, Montreal, Canada.

Luhr, William, editor, *World Cinema since 1945*, Ungar Pub Co, 1987.

MacDonald, J. F., *One Nation under Television: The Rise & Decline of Network TV*, Wadsworth Pub, 1994.

Mackaay, Ejan & Gendreau, Ysolde. *Canadian Legislation on Intellectual Property*. Carswell Pub, 2005.

Major League Baseball and the Major League Baseball Players' Association. NY, USA.

Mander, Jerry. *Four Arguments for the Elimination of Television*, Perennial 1978.

Mansion, H. *Tout le Monde Vous Dira Non: There is No Business Like Show Business*, Eds Stanké, 2005.

Marc, David. *Bonfire of Humanities: TV, Subliteracy & Long-Term Memory Loss,* Syracuse Univ Pr, 1995.

Marcus, Abraham and William, *Elements of Radio*, Prentice-Hall, 6th ed. 1972.

McGill University Faculty of Music, Marvin Duchow Music Library, Montreal, Quebec, Canada.

Media, Entertainment and Arts Alliance (MEAA), Australia.

Montreal Archives. Montreal, Quebec, Canada.

Montreal International Music Initiative (MIMI), Montreal, Canada.

Montreal Library/Bibliothèque de Montréal. Quebec, Canada.

Morton, David L. *Sound Recording : The Life Story of a Technology*, Greenwood Press, 2004.

Motion Picture Association of America (MPAA) & Motion Picture Association (MPA), Encino, Ca, USA.

Mottershead, Allen. *Introduction to electricity and electronics* radio waves, Prentice Hall, 3rd ed. 1990.

Moylan, William D., *The Art of Recording: The Creative Resources of Music Production and Audio; The Art of Recording: Understanding and Crafting the Mix.* Focal Press, 2002.

*Music Directory Canada*. Norris –Whitney Communications Inc Publishing, 8ᵗʰ ed., 2001.

Music Library Association (MLA), Middleton, WI, USA.

MusicFest Canada - North America's Largest Educational Music Festival, Richmond, BC, Canada.

National Academy of Recording Arts & Sciences (NARAS), Grammy Awards. Santa Monica, California.

National Archives & Public Record Office of England, Wales, UK. Kew, Richmond, Surrey, UK.

National Archives of Canada. Ottawa, Ontario, Canada.

National Archives, Washington, D.C., USA.

National Association of Theatre Owners, Washington DC, USA.

National Association for Retail Marketing Services (NARMS), Plover, Wisconsin, USA.

National Basketball League and the National Basketball League Players' Association.

National Football League and the National Football League Players' Association.

National Hockey League and the National Hockey League Players' Association.

National Library of Canada. Ottawa, Ontario, Canada.

National Music Publishers' Association (NMPA) & The Harry Fox Agency, Inc. (HFA), New York, USA.

Neighbouring Rights Collective of Canada (NRCC), Toronto, Canada.

*New Oxford History of Music*, 10 vol. (1954-90), various editors, Oxford University Press, 1995.

New York Public Library, New York City, NY, USA.

Newfoundland and Labrador Provincial Archives Division. St-John's, Newfoundland, Canada.

Nite, N. *Rock on Almanac: The First Four Decades of Rock 'N' Roll: A Chronology*, HarperCollins, 1989.

*North American Free Trade Agreement* (NAFTA), Canada, USA, Mexico.

North By Northeast Music Festival & Industry Conference (NXNE), Toronto, Canada.

Oelkers, Dotty. *Fashion Marketing,* South-Western Educational Pub, 2003.

Oldham, Gabriella. *First Cut: Conversations With Editors*, University of California Press, 1995.

Ontario Legislative Library. Toronto, Ontario, Canada.

Oxford University Libraries and Research Centers. Oxford, UK.

Pantuso, Joe, and Moss, Will, eds., *The Complete Internet Gamer*, 1996.

Passman, Don. *All You Need To Know About The Music Business.* Simon & Schuster, 5th edition, 2003.

Patterson, Lyman Ray. *Copyright in Historical Perspective.* Nashville: Vanderbilt University Pr., 1968; with S.W. Lindberg, *The Nature of Copyright: A Law of Users' Rights.* Athens: Univ. of Georgia Pr., 1991.

Periodical Writers Association of Canada (PWAC), Toronto, Ontario, Canada.

Playwrights Guild of Canada (PGC), Toronto, Ontario, Canada.

Plunket, E. M. , *Fashion,* Grolier, 1999.

Pomeroy, B. ed., *Beginnernet: A Beginner's Guide to the Internet and the World Wide Web,* Slack, 1997.

Poynter, Dan. *The Self-Publishing Manual: How to Write, Print, and Sell Your Own Book*, 14th Edition; Publishing Poynters Newsletter, 2005.

Prince Edward Island Public Archives and Records Office. Charlottetown, PEI, Canada.

Public Archives of Canada. Ottawa, Canada.

Public Archives of Nova Scotia. Halifax, Nova Scotia, Canada.

Public Lending Rights Commission (PLR), Ottawa, Canada.

Publishers Marketing Association (PWA), Manhattan Beach, California, USA.

Publishers Weekly, New York, USA.

Quebec Bar Association, Intellectual Property Section, Montreal Quebec, Canada.

Quebec City Library/Bibliothèque de Québec. Quebec City, Canada.

Quebec Federation of Musicians (QFM), Montreal, Canada.

Quebec Writers' Federation (QWF), Montreal, Canada.

Rader, B.G., *American Sports: From the Age of Folk Games to the Age of Televised Sports,* Prentice, 2003.

Randel, Don Michael (ed.), *The New Harvard Dictionary of Music.* Harvard University Press, 1986.

Recording Industry Association of America (RIAA), New York, USA.

Reid, R.H., *Architects of the Web: 1,000 Days that Built the Future of Business.* Wiley, 2nd edition, 1997.

Ro, Ronin, *...The Spectacular Rise and Violent Fall of Death Row Records*, Main Street Books, 1999.

Robinson, Deanna C. *Music at the Margins: Popular Music and Global Cultural Diversity.* Sage, 1991.

Romanowski, P., & George-Warren, H., eds., *The New Rolling Stone Encyclopedia of Rock n Roll.* 1995.

Rose, Mark, J. *Authors and Owners: The Invention of Copyright.* Harvard University Press, 1995; with Angela Adair-Hoy, *How To Publish and Promote Online*, St. Martin's Griffin, 2001.

Rothman, David. *Networld!: What People Are Really Doing on the Internet...,* Diane Pub, 1997.

Ryback, Timothy W. *Rock Around the Bloc: A History of Rock Music in Eastern Europe and the Soviet Union.* Oxford University Press, 1990.

Sadie, Stanley, ed., *The New Grove Dictionary of Music and Musicians*, 20 vols. 1980, repr. 1993, 3 vols. Macmillan, London, 1984; *Norton-Grove Concise Encyclopedia of Music.* Rev. ed. Norton, 1994.

Salzman, Eric. *Twentieth-century Music*, The Prentice Hall History of Music Series, 3rd ed. 1988.

Samuels, Edward. *The Illustrated Story of Copyright.* New York: St. Martin's Press, 2000.

Sanderson, Paul. *Musicians & the Law in Canada.* Carswell Publishing, 3rd Rev edition, 2000.

Schwartz, Daylle Deanna. *Start and Run Your Own Record Label.* Watson-Guptill Pub., 2003; *The Real Deal: How to Get Signed to a Record* Label, Billboard Books, updated edition, 2002.

Schwartz, Martin, *Radio Electronics Made Simple,* American Electronics Co, 1982.

Screen Actors' Guild (SAG), Los Angeles, USA.

Seuling, Barbara. *How to Write a Children's Book and Get It Published*, Wiley, 3rd edition, 2004.

Shakespeare Theatre Association of America (STAA).

Shemel, S. & Krasilovsky, W. *This Business of Music.* Billboard Books - Watson-Guptill Publishing, 9th ed.; *More About This Business of Music.* Billboard Books - Watson-Guptill Publishing, 5th edition, 1994.

Shrader, R. L., *Electronic Communication*, McGraw-Hill Science ,6th ed. 1991.

Shulman, B., et al., *The Beginner's Illustrated Internet Dictionary,* Bookworld Services, 1997.

Silverstein, Barry. *Business To Business Internet Marketing: Seven Proven Strategies for Increasing Profits Through Internet Direct Marketing, Maximum Press*, 4th ed., 2001.

Society for Reproduction Rights of Authors, Composers and Publishers in Canada (SODRAC), Montreal.

Society of Composers, Authors and Music Publishers of Canada (SOCAN), *Words & Music*, Toronto.

Society of European Stage Authors and Composers (SESAC), Nashville, Tennessee, USA.

Songwriters Association of Canada, (SAC), Toronto, Canada.

Songwriters Guild of America (SGA), New York, USA.

Squire, Jason, ed., *The Movie Business Book*, Fireside, 3rd edition, 2004.

Steele, Valerie, *Paris Fashion: A Cultural History* Oxford University Press, 1988; *Fifty Years of Fashion: New Look to Now*, Yale University Press, 2000.

Stefik, Mark, *Internet Dreams: Archetypes, Myths, and Metaphors*, The MIT Press, 1997.

Steingberg, Cobbett S. *TV Facts.* New York: Facts on File, 1980.

Stevens, Denis (editor), *A History of Song,* Greenwood Publishing, 1982.

Stevenson, Robert L., *Global Communication in the Twenty-First Century.* Allyn & Bacon, 1994.

Stolba, K Marie *The Development of Western Music: A History*, 2nd ed. Brown & Benchmark, 1994.

Stone, Elaine. *Fashion Merchandising: An Introduction*, Gregg Division McGraw-Hill; 5th ed. 1989.

Strong, Jeff. *Home Recording For Musicians For Dummies.* John Wiley & Sons, 2002.

Stuchly, Maria A. *Modern Radio Science,* Oxford University Press, 2002.

Summers, Jodi. *Making & Marketing Music: Musician's Guide to Financing, Distributing & Promoting Albums,* Allworth Press, 1999; *Moving Up in the Music Business*, Allworth Press, 2000; *Interactive Music Handbook:*

149

*The Definitive Guide to Internet Music Strategies, Enhanced CD Production and Business Development,* Watson-Guptill Publications, 1998.

Tanis, Nicholas. *Motion Picture,* 2000.

Tate, Sharon, and Edwards, Mona S., *Inside Fashion Design,* Prentice Hall, 5th edition, 2003.

Tebbel, John W. *History of Book Publishing in the US: The Great Change,* R.R. Bowker, 1981; *Between Covers: The Rise and Transformation of Book Publishing in America,* Oxford Univ. Pr. (Txt), 1987.

Telefilm Canada. Montreal, Canada.

Television Critics Association (TCA), Los Angeles, California, USA.

Tepper, Ron. *How to Get into the Entertainment Business : Behind-the-Scenes Jobs...,* Wiley, 1999.

Thall, Peter M., *What They'll Never Tell You About the Music Business: The Myths, Secrets, Lies (& a Few Truths).* Watson-Guptill Pub., 2002.

Thompson, Robert J., *Television's Second Golden Age,* Continuum Intl Pub Group, 1996; (editor) Television Studies: Textual Analysis (Media and Society Series), Praeger Publishers, 1989; with David Marc, *Television In The Antenna Age: A Concise History,* Blackwell Publishers, 2004; *Prime Time, Prime Movers: From I Love Lucy to L.A. Law-America's Greatest TV Shows and the People Who Created Them (The Television),* Syracuse University Press, Reprint edition (April 1, 1995).

Toronto Public Library. Toronto, Ontario, Canada.

*Trade Related Aspects of Intellectual Property Rights Agreement* (TRIPS), WTO 1986-94 Uruguay Round.

Trademarks Office, *Trademarks Journal/Act/Regulations/Examination Manual/Wares & Services Manual,* Canadian Intellectual Property Office, Industry Canada, Gatineau, Quebec, Canada.

Trebas Institute, Media Design & Technology College, Music Business Administration Program. Toronto, Ontario & Montreal, Quebec, Canada. David P. Leonard, President, CEO, founder.

*U.S. Digital Millennium Copyright Act* of 1998 *(DMCA).*

Underdown, Harold D. *Complete Idiot's Guide to Publishing Children's Books,* Alpha, 2001.

*Universal Copyright Convention* (U.C.C.), International Standards and Legal Affairs, UNESCO, 1971.

Université de Montréal, Facultés des arts et des sciences, Département d'histoire et l'art, *Les Grands courants de l'art - l'héritage occidental,* Professor Jean-François Lhote, 1988; U de M Libraries and Museums.

University of California, Los Angeles (UCLA), *Publishing Tomorrow: Catching New World Trends in the Book Business,* Professor Robert Windeler, 1991; UCLA Libraries and Museums, California. USA.

University of Missouri-Kansas City Archives, Kansas City, Missouri, USA.

*Uruguay Round General Agreement on Tariffs & Trade* (GATT), World Trade Organization (WTO), 1994.

Vaidhyanathan, Siva. *Copyrights and Copywrongs: The Rise of Intellectual Property and How It Threatens Creativity.* New York University Press, 2001.

Vanier College, Music Industry Seminars & Audio Recording Technology Program. Saint-Laurent, Qc, Cda.

Vinet, Mark. *Evolution of Modern Popular Music: A history of Blues, Jazz, Country, R&B, Rock and Rap* Wadem Publishing, 2004 (ISBN 0968832024), 117 Bellevue street, Vaudreuil-sur-le-Lac, Quebec, Canada, J7V-8P3. Tel: 450-510-1102 / 450-371-1803. Fax: 450-510-1095. mark@markvinet.com www.markvinet.com; *Authors' Moral Rights Under Section 12(7) of the Canadian Copyright Act,* Wadem Publishing, April 1987, McGill University, Faculty of Law, Montreal, Canada.

Visual Education Centre Limited. Etobicoke, Ontario, Canada.

Volanski, John J. *Sound Recording Advice: Manual That Demystifies the Home Recording Studio Experience,* Pacific Beach Pub, 2002.

Walker, J.R. and Ferguson, Douglas A. *The Broadcast Television Industry.* Boston: Allyn and Bacon, 1998.

Warner, Jay. *How to Have Your Hit Song Published,* Hal Leonard Corporation, 1988.

Westbrook, Alonzo. *Hip Hoptionary TM : The Dictionary of Hip Hop Terminology.* Harlem Moon, 2002.

Westrup, Jack A. *The New Oxford History of Music.* Oxford University Press, 1991.

Wharton, Brooke, *The Writer Got Screwed: Guide to the Legal and Business Practices of Writing for the Entertainment Industry,* HarperResource, 1997.

Whitaker, Jerry C., *Radio Frequency Transmission Systems: Design and Operation.* Mcgraw-Hill, 1991.

Wikipedia, *Podcasting, Ipods & MP3 (peer to peer); Radio formats,* 2005

Williams, R., *101 Music Business Contracts.* Platinum Millennium, 2001.

World Bk.; McClelland and Stewart; Funk & Wagnalls; Microsoft; Learning Co.; Britannica; Broderbund, Grolier; Interactive multimedia; International Photo & Images Copyright Clearances of New York.

World Intellectual Property Organization (WIPO), Agency of the United Nations; *WIPO Performances and Phonograms Treaty* (WPPT), Digital Millennium Copyright Act (DMCA), USA, 1998.

Writers Association for Resourceful Minds (WARM), Montreal, Canada.

Writers Guild of Canada (WGC), Toronto, Canada.

Writers Guild of America (WGA), New York, USA

Zollo, Paul. *Songwriters on Songwriting,* Da Capo Press, 4th edition, 2003.

# INDEX

## A

A&R (artist and repertoire), 64, 142
actor, 85-95, 97, 101-03, 121, 123-126, 129
agent, 60, 67, 73, 75, 78, 80-83, 103, 126, 140
Anton Pillar order, 40
art, 1-2, 4-6, 8, 21, 34-5, 49, 62, 65, 68, 73, 76, 86,
 91, 102, 116, 123, 127, 130, 134-36, 139, 141,
 143, 150
art dealer, 134, 136, 142
artist (performers), 7, 10-14, 15, 18, 24-25, 28, 33, 35,
 42, 44, 58, 64-65, 73, 86, 92, 94, 102-03, 116, 123,
 125-27, 130, 132, 136, 139, 147
ASCAP, 38, 144

## B

Berne Convention, 10, 20, 23-24, 31, 144
BMI, 38, 145
blogger, 113
book, 1-6, 8-13, 15-21, 29, 36, 40, 42, 48, 57, 59, 62,
 74-84, 87, 97, 109, 143
book club, 79
bookstore, 74, 82
broadcast, 19, 25, 32, 42, 62, 86, 95, 101, 110-11, 116
Broadway, 123, 125

## C

cable, 28, 86, 95, 100-01, 105, 110, 132
Canada, 2, 3, 9, 10, 13, 17-19, 22-25, 30-31, 33, 35-
 36, 110, 114, 129, 144-50
Canada United States Free Trade Agreement (FTA), 25
Canadian Copyright Act, 18, 150
Canadian Radio-television and Telecommunications
 Commission (CRTC), 110, 145
choreographer (phy), 20, 26, 31, 122-24, 141
cinematographer (phy), 26, 90, 94, 102, 141
circus, 123, 141
collective society, 36, 38, 71-72
compilation, 25-27, 30, 42
composer, 63, 68, 70-72, 87, 92, 97, 123-24, 140
computer, 16, 18, 20, 26-27, 33, 36, 40, 65, 78, 86,
 94-95, 113-17, 119-20, 136, 141, 146
concert, 20, 39, 73, 109, 140
confidential information and trade secrets, 14-17
consolidation, 79, 143
contract, 1-6, 8, 26, 55-57, 60-62, 70, 72, 73, 84, 89
convergence, 7-8, 10, 12, 79, 121, 143
copyright, 1-8, 10-11, 14-43, 55, 58, 62, 66, 68, 70-73,
 76, 82-83, 96, 105, 116-17, 130, 139, 141, 144-150
copyright infringement, 22, 25, 39-41, 49, 53, 116-17,
 130
costume designer, 90, 97, 99, 126-28, 136, 142
culture, 12-13, 129-30, 132-33, 138, 140

## D

designer, 68, 76, 78, 90, 94, 102, 123, 126-27, 130,
 133, 141
digital, 10, 12, 18, 20, 25-29, 34, 37, 42, 65, 78, 95,
 105, 108, 110, 116, 118, 141

Direct Broadcast Satellite (DBS), 111
director, 29, 85, 87-94, 97-100, 102-04, 106, 121-27,
 140-42, 146
director of photography (DP), 87, 90-92, 97, 142
distribution, 33, 63, 65, 73-74, 79, 85-86, 95, 97, 100,
 139
DVD, 16, 49, 66, 85-86, 96-97

## E

e-commerce, 3, 62, 73, 116, 141
editor, 78, 79, 80, 82, 83, 87, 91, 92, 97, 102, 104,
 140, 146, 148, 149, 150
electronics, 12, 148-49
endorsement, 63, 67, 131
Europe, 3, 38, 129, 149
European Union, 31

## F

fair dealings/use, 35
fashion, 1-2, 4-6, 8, 36, 128-30, 133, 135, 138, 141
Federal Communications Commissions (FCC), 110

## G

General Agreement on Tariffs and Trade (GATT), 25,
 150

## H

Hollywood, 86, 93, 145-47
homemade deposit, 14, 21-22

## I

illustration, 26, 29, 62, 68, 76, 135, 136, 141
industrial design, 14-16
injunction, 40, 53
integrated circuit topography, 14-16, 145
intellectual property, 2, 6, 9, 11, 14-17, 24-25, 44, 116,
 144-45, 147-50
Internet, 1-2, 4-6, 8, 10, 12, 18, 25, 28, 33-34, 42, 73,
 79, 86, 108, 110-11, 113-17, 119, 121, 131-33,
 145-50

## L

lawyer, 3, 8, 11, 45-46, 60, 62, 75, 80-82, 141

## M

Major League Baseball (MLB), 133
manager, 8, 30, 59, 60, 64, 70, 81, 87, 89, 93, 94, 97,
 102-03, 123-25, 133, 138, 140
manufacturing, 65, 78, 119, 138
marketing, 63, 74, 85, 108, 113, 118, 128, 139
merchandising, 1-2, 4-6, 8, 62-63, 73, 86, 95, 130-32,
 136-39, 142, 149
moral rights, 31-34, 37, 39

movie (film), 1-2, 4-6, 8, 12-13, 16, 20-21, 23, 26, 28-29, 36, 45, 53, 59, 66, 71-73, 79, 84-99, 101, 103, 117, 121, 125, 129-30, 132-33, 136, 140-42, 144-48, 150

MP3, 72, 150

multimedia, 66, 113, 115, 144, 150

music, 1-6, 8, 13, 21, 25, 28-29, 36, 38, 40, 45, 48, 56, 61, 63, 64, 66-68, 70-73, 79, 87, 92, 97, 101, 104-05, 109, 116-17, 121, 123, 129, 130, 132, 135-36, 139, 140-41, 144-50

musician, 60, 64, 65, 67, 73, 104, 124

**N**

National Basketball Association (NBA), 133

National Football League (NFL), 133

National Hockey League (NHL), 133

neighboring rights, 24, 32-33, 35

North American Free Trade Agreement (NAFTA), 25, 148

**O**

Olympic Games, 132-33, 147

**P**

painting, 19, 26, 135

patent, 14-16, 145-46

peer-to-peer, 40, 116, 150

photograph, 21, 26, 29, 31, 34, 36, 42, 62, 68, 73, 76, 83, 91, 115, 130

piracy, 39, 116

plagiarism, 39

playwright, 122-23, 124, 125, 140

podcasting, 111, 113, 150

producer, 24-25, 28-29, 33, 35, 41, 44, 64, 66, 86-89, 91-95, 97, 99, 100-104, 106, 108, 122-126, 141

publisher/publishing, 2-3, 6, 8, 12, 17, 20, 30, 37-38, 40, 64, 67-84, 144, 146-50

**R**

radio, 1-6, 8, 23, 28, 33, 66, 108-12, 115-16, 121, 132-33, 141, 148

record label, 6, 63-69, 73, 130, 149

recording, 2, 3, 19, 20, 22, 24, 28, 31-36, 39, 42, 56, 61, 63-66, 68-70, 73, 92, 94, 102, 104-05, 125, 141

recreation, 8, 132, 143

reproduction/mechanical rights, 19, 21, 35-39, 42, 62, 70

retailer, 7, 41, 63, 65, 74, 79, 95, 118, 137-38

Rome Convention, 24, 147

**S**

sampling, 28, 140

satellite, 9, 28, 85-86, 95, 100-01, 105, 108, 110-11, 132

screenwriter (script), 29, 87-90, 93-94, 97-99, 100-03, 105-06 125, 127

singer, 64, 67-68, 124, 125

SOCAN, 38, 149

software, 17, 113-16, 118-20, 142

Songwriters Association of Canada (SAC), 23, 149

sound engineer (audio professional), 64, 66, 68, 73, 92, 102, 104, 142

soundtrack (musical scores), 25, 92, 94

special effects, 85, 91-92, 94-95, 98-99, 101, 104-05, 126, 142

sponsorship, 63, 67, 131

sports, 1-2, 4-6, 8, 82, 101, 109, 120, 130, 131-33, 142, 144

Statute of Anne, 17

studio, 57, 59, 63, 65-66, 68, 73, 85-90, 92-93, 96, 98, 101, 126, 130, 141-42, 150

Super Bowl, 133

**T**

technology, 12, 16, 18, 40, 66, 95-96, 101, 110, 116, 120, 127, 142

television, 1-2, 4-6, 8, 12, 16, 23, 28, 33, 36, 66, 73, 79, 84, 86, 93, 95, 97, 100-07, 110-11, 115-16, 119, 121, 125, 129, 130, 132-33, 136, 142, 145, 147-50

theater, 1-2, 4-6, 8, 45, 73, 86, 95, 122-27, 132, 136, 141

trademark, 1-2, 4-6, 8, 10-11, 14-16, 26, 44-55, 62, 73, 83, 130, 133, 138-39, 141

trademark agent, 44-46

treaty country, 10, 20

**U**

United Nations, 24, 49

United States of America (USA), 2-3, 9, 10, 13, 17-19, 22-23, 25, 30-31, 34-36, 38, 77, 110, 114, 129, 130, 138, 144, 146-49

United States Copyright Act, 17

United States Copyright Office, 22

Universal Copyright Convention (UCC), 10, 20, 23-24, 150

**V**

video games, 1-2, 4-6, 8, 13, 73, 79, 118-21, 132

**W**

website, 21, 25, 27, 29, 40, 42, 73, 82, 141

wholesaler, 7, 61, 138, 141

WIPO Performances and Phonograms Treaty, 25, 150

work-made-for-hire, 30-31

World Intellectual Property Organization (WIPO), 24, 25, 144, 146, 150

World Series, 133

World Trade Organization (WTO), 10, 20, 25, 150

World Wide Web (WWW), 115-16, 149

writer, 3, 8-12, 17, 19-21, 23, 26-35, 38-39, 43, 70-72, 74-84, 87, 92, 101, 103, 144-45, 147, 149-50

Writers Guild of America, 23, 150

Writers Guild of Canada, 23, 150

MEMBER OF SCABRINI GROUP

Québec, Canada
2007